Forever Faithful

Dogs That Return

First published by O Books, 2009
O Books is an imprint of John Hunt Publishing Ltd., The Bothy, Deershot Lodge, Park Lane, Ropley,
Hants, SO24 0BE, UK
office1@o-books.net
www.o-books.net

Distribution in:	South Africa
	Alternative Books
UK and Europe	altbook@peterhyde.co.za
Orca Book Services	Tel: 021 555 4027 Fax: 021 447 1430
orders@orcabookservices.co.uk	
Tel: 01202 665432 Fax: 01202 666219	Text copyright Jenny Smedley 2008
Int. code (44)	
	Design: Stuart Davies
USA and Canada	
NBN	ISBN: 978 1 84694 174 0
custserv@nbnbooks.com	
Tel: 1 800 462 6420 Fax: 1 800 338 4550	All rights reserved. Except for brief quotations
	in critical articles or reviews, no part of this
Australia and New Zealand	book may be reproduced in any manner without
Brumby Books	prior written permission from the publishers.
sales@brumbybooks.com.au	
Tel: 61 3 9761 5535 Fax: 61 3 9761 7095	The rights of Jenny Smedley as author have
	been asserted in accordance with the
Far East (offices in Singapore, Thailand,	Copyright, Designs and Patents Act 1988.
Hong Kong, Taiwan)	
Pansing Distribution Pte Ltd	
kemal@pansing.com	A CIP catalogue record for this book is available
Tel: 65 6319 9939 Fax: 65 6462 5761	from the British Library.

Printed by Digital Book Print

O Books operates a distinctive and ethical publishing philosophy in
all areas of its business, from its global network of authors to
production and worldwide distribution.
This book is produced on FSC certified stock, within ISO14001
standards. The printer plants sufficient trees each year through
the Woodland Trust to absorb the level of emitted carbon in
its production.

Forever Faithful

Dogs That Return

Jenny Smedley

BOOKS

Winchester, UK
Washington, USA

CONTENTS

This book is dedicated to my dog, Ace.
She was (is) the best dog that ever lived – again and again.
This is her true story.

I died as a mineral and became a plant,
I died as a plant and rose to animal,
I died as animal and I was man.
Why should I fear?
When was I less by dying?
Jalalu 'D-Din Rumi, Sufi poet

He is your friend, your partner, your defender, your dog.
You are his life, his love, his leader. He will be yours, faithful and true,
to the last beat of his heart. You owe it to him to be worthy of such
devotion.
Unknown

A dog is the only thing on this earth that loves you more than he loves
himself.
Josh Billings (Henry Wheeler Shaw)

You think dogs will not be in heaven?
I tell you, they will be there long before any of us.
Robert Louis Stevenson
The Power of the Dog

There is sorrow enough in the natural way
From men and women to fill our day;
And when we are certain of sorrow in store,
Why do we always arrange for more?
Brothers and sisters, I bid you beware
Of giving your heart to a dog to tear.

Buy a pup and your money will buy
Love unflinching that cannot lie—
Perfect passion and worship fed
By a kick in the ribs or a pat on the head.
Nevertheless it is hardly fair
To risk your heart to a dog to tear.

When the fourteen years which Nature permits
Are closing in asthma, or tumor, or fits,
And the vet's unspoken prescription runs
To lethal chambers or loaded guns,
Then you will find—it's your own affair—
But ... you've given your heart to a dog to tear.

When the body that lived at your single will,
With its whimper of welcome, is stilled (how still!)
When the spirit that answered your every mood
Is gone—wherever it goes—for good,
You will discover how much you care,
And will give your heart to a dog to tear.

We've sorrow enough in the natural way,
When it comes to burying Christian clay.
Our loves are not given, but only lent,
At compound interest of cent per cent.
Though it is not always the case, I believe,
That the longer we've kept 'em, the more do we grieve:
For, when debts are payable, right or wrong,
A short-term loan is as bad as a long—
So why in—Heaven (before we are there)
Should we give our hearts to a dog to tear?

Rudyard Kipling

Introduction

The poem, *The Power of the Dog*, by Rudyard Kipling, says it all, because dogs do have the power to break our hearts. We have taken them out of the wild and domesticated them, changed them, even redesigned them in some cases, and because of this we have to take on a huge burden of responsibility for their lives, and the sadness, in the end, when they leave this earth plane.

Dogs don't live as long as people, so once you do take on that responsibility of bringing a dog into your world, you may well find yourself having many dogs during your lifetime.

You pick up that cute puppy, and take him into your heart and your home. It all seems to be idyllic at that point; there are years and years of happy companionship stretching out ahead of you. It can seem as if it will be endless, but sadly it isn't. Each one will leave you at some point when they come to the end of their lifespan.

First there's the puppy-hood, full of sleepless nights, accident-ridden carpets, chewed furniture, excited playing and adorable cuddles. Then comes the training, the bonding, as your dog, at about three years old, enters his teenage equivalent years. You're so proud as your dog starts to grasp a vocabulary, understanding many words as he interprets what you want him to do, and learns tricks, to shake a paw, roll over, kiss. But eventually just 10 or 12 years down the line, they enter their doggy old age, and your heart starts to contract as you notice he's not so quick anymore and his muzzle is starting to look grizzled, and his eyes dimmer. His hearing starts to fade, and you know deep down, that it won't be many more years before you're called on to make the ultimate sacrifice.

I call it the ultimate sacrifice, because that's what it is, it's making the decision to sacrifice your beloved companion, for his own sake. It's never going to be for your sake. Dogs that are loved, entwine themselves inextricably around your heart, so when you love your dog, letting him go is far harder for you than for him. If dogs can't be dogs, then they have nothing. Being a dog means having keen eyesight and hearing, and an even keener sense of smell. It means rejoicing in food, in your pack's company, in chasing down smells and running after prey, even if it's only pretend prey. Your dog can't amuse himself by reading a book or watching TV. If he is in pain or discomfort, he can't listen to music to relax in the way you can as you get older. He can't find comfort in his old age in the ways you can, and so, inevitably the dreaded day comes, that, barring accidents or sudden acute illness, you will have to arrange. It's not fair to keep an unhappy dog alive just because you don't want to feel the pain of parting. You'll owe it to him to make that call.

After the grief of the moment, comes the guilt, as you ask yourself searching questions. *Should I have ended his life? Could I have done something different?* You think *I can't do this again.* Yet the absence of your dear friend and constant companion is so hard to bear. You can't stand the thought of trying to replace your friend, because it would seem such a betrayal, and yet, there is such emptiness in your house when you come home alone, with no tail wagging in greeting, no whining hello, none of the old excitement that proved that you, above all other humans, are the most beloved of all.

I have come to understand that this terrible parting can sometimes be rectified.

There is more to this relationship we have with our dogs than just the remembered comfort and companionship of keeping warm together at the fireside, inherited from our ancestors. There is there a deeper connection between this descendent of the wolf and jackal, and humans, than most of us realize. Can we draw out this relationship and make the partnership less transient? Or perhaps it really is less transient than it seems, and we just don't realize it.

Our relationship with dogs as with all animals, especially the domesticated ones, starts at soul level. But dogs share our homes and our lives. More than that, some special dogs are a reflection of their owners, and some very special ones share a facet of our soul with us. These are the dogs that we speak of as being 'almost human', those that seem to be able to reason, who are self-aware, and can make sentient decisions. These dogs are forever connected to us with a link that cannot be broken, and when they die they tear a part of their owner's spirit out.

Does this mean that there's any comfort to be had at all in their passing? Yes, I believe there is. What if you knew that your dog could come back to you in another body? What if you knew that your dog had come back to you before in other lifetimes, and will do so again? What if you had incontrovertible proof that your dog had returned to you in a new body?

These miracles happen every day, all over the world, with special dogs, and they do give us comfort, because they demonstrate that this facet of your soul is forever faithful, and will return time and time again to be reunited with you.

Dogs come back. Dogs reincarnate, and special dogs return to that special owner over and over again. If you have one of these special dogs in your life, and if you can embrace the concept that he has come back to you, not just this once but many times, you'll be able to regress to relive other lifetimes you've spent together.

When this happened to me, it made me completely re-evaluate the journey that we and our dogs share together. The body my reincarnated dog is in now is called KC, but before that she was Ace. Once I had accepted that our amazing multiple life bond was a fact, I was able to communicate with her on a soul level, and find out about what happened to her before she came to me in this life, and I was able to understand the very difficult journey she'd undertaken to be with me again. I came to realize that a dog like this can actually be a spark of your own soul, a spiritual mentor and friend, coming along with you through your lives, to help you find your way.

Dog-training manuals show you how to control your dog and teach him to do tricks. What I want to show you is how you can trigger and develop a much deeper relationship with your special dog, one that will not only give you amazing control over his behaviour, by being so in tune with him, but you'll also enhance and develop your own personality on a spiritual level.

Your dog has knowledge of you that you yourself don't have. By accessing this knowledge, you'll come to understand that you and your special dog can be part of one unified soul, and there is no closer bond. This bond, if you can achieve it, can also actually influence your life too. It can make you a more balanced, and therefore a much happier, person.

CHAPTER 1

My Dog's Story Begins

The skinny, black puppy tried to make herself as small as possible, curling into a tight ball, her tail wrapped around her nose, and her paws tucked in. When her humans were shouting at each other, it was always the best thing to do, as it made her less of a target. The puppy was terrified, but the house was rarely calm except during the long, long hours when no-one was home. Although she relished the peace and quiet at those lonely times, the puppy was always worried that she might have an 'accident'. If she did make a mess, which was often, despite holding it in for so long that her belly hurt, once the couple returned, she'd get a hefty wallop at the very least, no matter how much she groveled and apologized.

She'd be lucky to escape her nose being roughly rubbed in the offending mess too. On one occasion after he came home to a mess, the man had lit a cigarette and held its glowing end to her paw, making her jerk back, yelping in pain. From that day on, if she saw the matchbox opened and a stick from it flaring into miniature fire, she would go and hide. On another occasion, the woman had chased the puppy into a corner with the vacuum cleaner, so that she could give her a whack. The puppy had been wary of that household machine ever since.

Rarely, the man and woman were quiet when they were home, and they heated up a ready-meal or a takeaway in the microwave, which they ate from plates balanced precariously on their laps, while they stared blankly at the flickering TV screen as it babbled away in the corner. While they dished up the meal, the puppy, always hungry, would sit under the table, drooling over the delicious smells that wafted around the kitchen. The couple would usually down a few bottles of beer too, and then mellowed out, they'd give the puppy some food scraps. The spicy foods made her tongue and gums burn a bit, but she'd become used to it. More often than not, though, the humans weren't quiet, and her ears were hurt by screeching and banging as their return home signaled an argument. Sometimes, like today, it turned out she had chosen the wrong place to hide, and she was hurled right into the middle of their battle.

The first warning signs that this was going to be one of the bad times had come as the pair of humans had entered the house already shouting at each other. Then they started arguing over boiling the kettle for a cup of tea. They often argued violently about trivial things like whether the milk should go in the cup first, or had the one who made the tea left the tea-bags in too long. Heeding the early warning signs, the pup had crept across the faded, flowery kitchen flooring, and hidden. Now the argument had escalated, and the man was shouting ever louder, the woman was screaming shrilly, and both of them were throwing things around the kitchen. The china and saucepans were crashing to the ground, the plates and cups smashing into pieces on the scruffy linoleum floor, and shattering against the chipped wall tiles.

On this occasion it soon became apparent the pup had chosen badly. She'd curled up behind the ragged green and white gingham curtain that blocked off the under-sink space. Jammed in amongst the dustpans and bottles, she peered through rips in the cloth at the warring couple, pungent smells of bleach and other chemicals over-stimulating her sensitive nose, whiffs passing headily through her nostrils. She snuffed unhappily to herself, trying not to sneeze and give her hiding place away, and scrunched herself up even more. But suddenly, a china plate flew towards the pup, skimming across the lino, smashing to the floor right under her nose. As the plate shattered into half a dozen pieces, shards pinging off her face, she was unable to stop herself, and she jumped out of her hiding place with a yelp. The sound and sight of her flying out from under the sink triggered an angry response from the man.

"You! You little rat! C'mere!" he yelled as he spotted her, an obvious and vulnerable scapegoat to vent his temper tantrum on. The man was giving off wave after wave of aggressive energy, which hit the puppy like a sledgehammer, galvanizing her into flight. She scrambled across the lino towards the door to the hallway, but her way was blocked by the woman, who was equally angry and also looking for something to take it out on. Hands grabbed at her as the pup skidded to a halt, her feet slithering on the grubby lino. Claws frantically digging for grip, she turned and ran back, diving beneath the wooden table. There was nowhere else to go. The man and woman circled the table, and this was a most dangerous sign. When they joined forces, united in a single cause, they could be very cruel. The puppy shivered and backed up as far as she could go. The man bent over, peering under the table, his face in shadow, while the murky sunlight from the window made a glowing halo of his spiky, pale crew-cut. His ear-ring sparkled and the sun lit up the eagle tattoo on his neck. Something glinting and shiny was in his hand. It might have been the pup's tin-can food bowl, and feeling a sudden, irrepressible surge of hungry happiness, she moved slightly nearer to the man's legs, her mouth-watering.

"Dinner, come on," said the man cajolingly.

Maybe, just maybe, this time things were going to be different. But the puppy's flash of joy was short-lived. Water shot out of the shiny object and cascaded towards her. As it hit her chest and one front leg the puppy squealed in pain. The water burnt her. It was scalding hot, straight from the boiled kettle.

Her skin screamed as the water penetrated her thin fur, and the puppy ran out from under the table. She noticed that the woman had moved away from the kitchen door and she ran for it, squeezing between the door edge and the jamb, yowling. The woman flung out an arm and the door crashed shut, but it was too late. The puppy had skimmed through the narrowing gap, and she careened down the hallway, ruffling up the balding carpet under her wildly paddling feet, and still crying from the sting. Her heart leapt when she saw that the front door was ajar. Daylight beckoned, its lacy beams threading through a yellowing, flapping net curtain, and highlighting the millions of dust motes that floated in the light like tiny golden sparks.

The man and woman had been so angry when they came into the house that they hadn't bothered to shut the door properly. The puppy ran to it, and hooked a paw into the two inch gap, pulling it wider. She slithered through, and catapulted down the front path. Her speed and momentum carried her out of the garden, right across the pavement, startling an elderly lady pulling a shopping trolley, and out into the middle of the road. She stopped for a second as the sunlight dazzled her and the noise of the traffic deafened her. The world was a bright cacophony that hurt her eyes and ears. It was complete sensory overload and for a moment it held her frozen.

The puppy had never been outdoors before, apart from her daily excursions around the dark, smelly back yard. That place was damp and full of shadows, however hard the sun shone. A row of shaggy, overgrown Cypress leylandii trees towered over it, blotting out any attempt by the sun to warm the concrete patch. The cracked, buckling surface was damp and moldy and covered with moss. There were broken beer bottles in one corner and soggy cardboard scattered around, but it was the only outside space the pup had ever known. Now, out in the big wide world, she stared around, blinking, unable to move. Then the front door flew open and the man and woman emerged, still yelling, the offending kettle gripped in the man's hand.

The puppy was transfixed with terror for a moment, and then a loud horn blared right behind her, and she spun away from the sound, running right down the centre of the road. A huge metal monster pursued her and her heart stuttered in terror. The car squealed and screeched as the driver slammed on the brakes, and a dark threatening shadow was cast over the puppy. Nothing had hit her though, and she could hear shouts behind her, and frightening, clashing noises. She didn't think the man and woman would chase after her but she didn't want to take the chance, so she just kept running as fast as she could.

She ran down the road from the terraced house she had been born in, where her mother had suddenly vanished from, and where her brothers and sisters had gradually been sold. Spindly trees and scrubby bushes flashed past in her peripheral vision, as her mind took her away from the terror of the monster on her heels, and she remembered how it had once been. Her mother had been a beautiful black Labrador and her father a black and tan German Shepherd. The puppy had been really happy for the first few weeks after she was born. She'd had her mum to cuddle and feed from. She'd enjoyed the delicious taste of warm milk gurgling down her throat. She'd had her brothers and sisters to play with and wrestle with, and nestle against in wonderful sleep. But things had changed drastically in her eighth week.

It was the most terrible time of loss. Her mother had been put on her lead one day, taken out, and had never come back. The pup had cried for her long into the night, before she finally settled down in the furry pile that was all of her family, being glad that at least she had them for warmth. Then people started visiting the house, picking up her brothers and sisters one at a time, and gradually her siblings had vanished, carried away in the arms of cooing couples. The nights got lonelier and chillier as they went, until the pup was the only one left. The night the last one of her siblings went she was in a state of shock. She waited and hoped for another couple to turn up and take her away as well, but they never came. Then her real and horrible life had started. For the past two weeks, she had learnt that fate was harsh and unfair, and that her life was barely worth living.

She ran on and on down the road, the car slowly tailing her, and it took her a long time to figure that if she went over to the squared off pathway at the side, the car wouldn't follow her. She eventually realized, and took to the pavement. Then she ran around a corner, knowing that she was running for her life. If the man and woman caught her this time, she knew it would be the end of her. Her life might have been miserable, but still her survival instinct kicked in. She reached the end of the next road and without hesitating, turned left just because the trees there looked a bit greener and a bit healthier. She went along another road, around another corner, along another road, turned again, always putting more and more space between herself and her past.

Noises came at her from all directions, and acrid smells constantly assaulted her nose. Whenever she crossed a street, cars screeched at her and brakes squealed, everything sounding so loud to her ears. Suddenly she came face to face with a two-wheeled machine, with a boy on board, and this one was on the paved path. For a second she thought the rubber wheel was going to run right into her, and closed her eyes tightly, but the machine swerved at the last moment, and crashed to the ground. The boy fell off, and then sprang to his feet, lunging at her and shouting after her as she ran away.

Occasionally people on foot shouted at her too, and often they made a grab at her, but no-one touched her and nothing hit her. Instinctively, she followed her ears' directions, constantly turning away from noise, into quieter and quieter areas. The noises faded and began to die away. Spotting a small back lane she whipped down it, into sudden peace, tranquility and shady corners. As her weariness grew, her fear diminished, and her frantic gallop turned into a steady trot. Gradually, her eyes stopped bugging out of her head and she became a bit more aware of her surroundings. She could hear the sounds of cars in the distance, but they were muffled by brickwork.

Finally, 30 minutes after her flight had started, the exhausted puppy gradually slowed down to a walk, and then she stopped, panting. She looked back. By now she was in a quiet access road that ran behind a terraced row of houses, with only the back yards of the houses facing it, and no-one was about. She didn't know what to do with this strange new life she'd run to. She wanted to sit down, lie down, and have her mother lick her skin where the water had touched her and scalded her, but it wasn't going to happen. She wanted a cool drink, but there was none. Even though she had never before left the house she was born in, in her whole life, all ten weeks of it, she knew that her only option was to find shelter, before another human got hold of her. Maybe next time, she wouldn't escape with her life. To her, humans were the scariest creatures on earth.

After skulking down the road for a while, the puppy saw a row of black dustbins at the side, next to a comfortingly solid, wooden fence. She crept into the void behind the bins and lay down in the dust to inspect her wounds. The skin under the black fur was red and swollen. It smarted. The pup licked it as best she could, though her tongue was dry from thirst and just wanted to pant the heat out of her body. She couldn't reach the sore places on her chest, no matter how she tried.

It was August, and a balmy, early evening, so at least she wasn't cold. The dustbins smelt temptingly of food, but they were tall wheelie bins, and there seemed to be no way she could get to what was inside them. She stood up on her hind legs, and despite the pain it caused, she reached up a dustbin as high as she could with her front paws. They slid and scraped down the bin's plastic sides, and she realized it was no use. She needed water, she needed food, and she needed, above all else, to feel safe. The sun was still quite high in the sky, and she thought she'd just lie down for a little while. Her head started to sag almost immediately, as exhaustion took over. Her head steadily drooped towards the dusty ground, and when it settled there, dirt smudging her nose, its gritty smell filling her nostrils, she never even realized it was happening. Healing sleep overcame her. As the air cooled, it soothed her sore skin a little bit and she fell into a deeper sleep. She slept on all through the night, unmoving.

CHAPTER 2

Learning to Live

The next morning the puppy was woken suddenly by a terrifying, grinding, clamoring noise. For a second she thought she was back in the house again, but her nose soon told her she was still outside. She peered fearfully around the bins she'd hidden behind. There was a giant vehicle inching down the lane towards her. Its huge sets of massive wheels rolled round and round. Men were jumping on and off the vehicle, carrying the bins from further up the road. The bins were lifted by machine arms and tipped high into the air, and the rubbish cascaded down into the back of the truck. The puppy was too scared to move, so she waited while the bins nearest to her were taken, emptied into the yawning maw, and then replaced, thinking she would creep behind them before hers were moved, and that way no-one would see her. But as soon as she moved, her burnt skin, which had shrunk and tightened overnight, split apart, and the awful agony of it made her scream.

The dustman who had just been about to pick up the bin that concealed her, drew back in alarm at the sudden shriek, and then peered gingerly behind it. "Oh my God, it's a dog, a puppy. It's hurt." He cooed softly, and reached down with big gloved hands to scoop her up. But the pup was too scared to let him touch her. He sounded gentle, but so had the 'man' on occasions. She'd been fooled before and wasn't about to be tricked into falling back into anyone's hands again. She flew from behind the bin, ignoring her pain, and ran away from the dustman as fast as she could. A thick conifer hedge a few yards away caught her eye, and she scrambled underneath it, pushing through prickly needles, out into the back yard that lay beyond. The yard reminded her of the one at the house she'd lived in, except it wasn't rank with the stench of feces and stale urine, it was quite bright, with tubs of flowers, and a white plastic table and chairs. But there was nothing to eat or drink, so she needed to move on. She shook herself tiredly, and pine needles flew from her coat. The smell of them was interesting, and she snuffed at them, but the needles weren't edible.

Luckily for her, there was a dividing alleyway between the backs of the houses ahead of her, otherwise she would have been trapped. She ran down one of them, through the darkness, and then stopped at the end, just short of the splashes of sunlight that poked their warm fingers into the alleyway. She peered fearfully out from the cold, dark, but concealing, passageway. She couldn't see or hear anyone out there, so she walked on, into the full light of the sunny front garden, feeling exposed.

She forgot her fear for a moment when miracle of miracles, she saw an old, empty, crisp packet laying there on the scraggy grass, sparkling with diamond droplets of precious water. She ran her tongue over it, slurping the small pool of water into her mouth. It was delicious. Then she paused just long enough to lick the salt from the wrapper – another thing she instinctively knew she needed. She carried on chewing the cellophane packet, not wanting to give it up, until the sharp tang of the ink from the printing on it made her spit it out. Then on she went, with no idea what to do next. Her small, scrawny belly growled with hunger. She moved out of the garden through the open gap between the red brick garden walls, and out onto the pavement. Still there was no sign of any other life, and that suited her just fine.

Her paws were sore from their unaccustomed exercise the previous day, and before long she was limping. Soon she came across a busier area and a small group of schoolboys spotted her. They may have had nice enough intentions, but she was filled with fear when they tried to trap her, circling round her, holding out their arms to block her escape. She tore through a gap and ran across some grass that divided up a car park's spaces. The grass was long and tufty, and her tired legs almost let her down, but she made it to a patch of waste ground, diving under a very prickly bramble bush. The boys gave chase, calling out to her. They surrounded the bush where she'd gone to ground. They first tried to reach her where she cowered, but she kept backing up, going deeper and deeper, despite the spiteful thorns that caught in her coat and threatened to tear her skin. Not able to reach her with their hands, the boys fetched a long stick and tried to force her to come out by pushing it towards her. But it wasn't long enough. At the back of the bramble bush the ground became ever rougher, with deeper cover, so finally the boys admitted defeat, knowing they had to go or be late for school.

The pup stayed in her hiding place for a long time after the last boy had gone, until finally some fabulous, mouth-drooling smells wafting on a breeze, drew her out. Extricating herself from the brambles with some difficulty, eyes tightly shut to avoid the thorns, she followed her nose back across the car park and into a small shopping arcade. She tracked the tempting smell to a doorway oozing aromas that made her tummy growl even louder. She crouched to one side, while the enticing, wafting smells that came through the door struggled to overcome her fear that there would be people inside. The smell was sweet, sugary and warm, fresh bread competing with iced doughnuts. Winning the fight, her nose twitched as she gave in to it and she poked her head around the corner. She was immediately spotted by a merry-looking lady in a white overall, who smiled broadly at her. The puppy froze, not knowing whether to retreat or see what happened. Her nose won again, and she stood her ground, trembling.

"Aw, look," the woman turned and called out towards the back room, "We've got an adorable little customer here." She plucked a crumbly, hot sausage roll from under a glass counter and held it towards the puppy, "Come on sweetheart, I won't hurt you."

The puppy's lips drooled, as the sausage meat called to her, and chains of dribble fell from her chin. It was irresistible. She inched forwards and opened her mouth. Her tiny, white, pin-like teeth clamped onto the sausage roll and she closed her eyes in ecstasy. It was the best thing she'd ever tasted. The baker's assistant let go of the roll and cautiously reached down.

Just as her hands were about to close around the puppy's bony body, someone shouted right next to her, "Oi! What d'you think you're doin!"

The pup opened her eyes, tightened her grip on the sausage roll, and turned tail, as the mouth, in the big red face of the baker, opened and shouted again. The assistant's mouth was a big 'O' of surprise and her eyes were wide as she made a quick grab for the dog, but the puppy scuttled around, puff pastry flakes flying in all directions, and bolted. She ran out of the door and around the corner, diving behind a large, wheeled bin. She crouched there and ravenously devoured the sausage roll. She could hear the baker and his assistant arguing, and their raised voices were scary, but she had to stay until she'd eaten every last scrap of her delicious prize.

Over the next two weeks the puppy learned who to approach and who to avoid. Females were usually the best bet, and she managed to scrounge just enough food from the various shops to keep herself alive. Butcher's assistants got used to her appearing every day, begging for a bone or some scraps of raw meat, and mostly they threw her something. People tried to catch her as the more caring among them could see that she was in urgent need of veterinary treatment, and was obviously homeless, but the puppy's wits grew with her experiences and she was impossible for them to get hold of.

Water was sometimes more of a problem than food, but she managed to find just enough to keep going, in buckets, in puddles and gutters, or on the leaves of bushes, or on drain covers. But she was gradually getting weaker. Hunger and thirst made her muscles lax, and the burns were more painful than ever. They'd turned into huge abscesses that throbbed more and more as they got bigger. People started to get much closer to catching her as her reflexes got slower. Unbeknownst to her, the police had been informed about her poor state, and they were daily ever closer to catching her too.

There came the time when one morning she couldn't get up from her hiding place for some time, and if anyone had come across her at that moment, she would have been helpless. She was so tired of struggling to live. She thought life was slipping away from her, whatever she did, and her thirst was getting worse and worse. She stopped trying to get up and just subsided to the ground. She'd found a pile of broken up polystyrene packaging the night before, and it made a nice, warm bed. She just wanted to sleep. She closed her eyes again, content to just give up and drift away forever.

Then she lifted her head. She could smell water. Her nose wrinkled at it because it didn't smell quite right and there was something odd about it, but it *was* water. It made her dry mouth and throat plead to be taken to it, but she didn't dare try and go to the water during the day, because she was so weak that she could easily have been caught. She rested during that day, slumped on her make-shift bed, collecting her reserves for one last effort. When it got dark and there were fewer people about, she slowly followed her trusty nose again, and it led her across Great Yarmouth town and onto the beach. Her paws sunk into the soft sand, making walking difficult in her weakened state, but when she crested a slight rise, she could hardly believe her eyes. There, right in front of her was miles and miles of water, cool, clean water. She walked towards it, hypnotized and puzzled by its 'to and fro' movement.

Once she reached it, the water alternately trickled over her toes and then drew back away from her. She sniffed the water. It still smelt weird, but her thirst forcefully overcame her caution.

She waded in, up to her distended belly, and after an initial sting, the salt water started to sooth her burns. She sank her nose into the water and started to drink. It tasted funny too. It was salty, but it was cold and good and it slaked her thirst. Some instinct told her to stop, that the water was bad, but she couldn't. A few minutes later she staggered from the water with a full, swollen belly, and flopped down on the sand, which was still warm from the sun, and fell asleep.

In the morning, this was where a kind lady found her. The pup tried to run when she felt hands picking her up, but her body was limp, her muscles were weak, and she couldn't struggle any more. She was barely breathing. She closed her eyes and gave up the fight. She remained out cold as the woman carried her off, put her inside a cage in the back of a white van, drove her through the town, took her inside a white room and placed her inside a small cage on a bed of warm, fluffy, white bedding. She never stirred when a vet arrived and examined her, and an intravenous drip was attached to one paw. She lay like the dead while the local anesthetic was applied and the abscesses were drained and bandaged. The woman and the vet wondered if the puppy would survive the night.

CHAPTER 3

A Dog of my Own

In our Norfolk farmhouse that night, my husband, Tony, and I were thinking that we could and should offer a home to another dog. We already had two dogs. Nyssa was a black collie cross spaniel, and Peri was a ginger and white, fuzzy-coated, Jack Russell collie cross. We had plenty of land at the time, and we always liked to offer a home to rescue dogs, rather than pay vast amounts of money for pedigree breeds, which were often unhealthy. Cross-breed mongrels had the added superior immune system that comes from mixing the genes of two or more breeds. We also preferred to give homes to the unwanted ones. It was a nice and healthy pastime to walk them round the field every day, or along the local footpaths, and neither of us could imagine not having a selection of dogs to enrich our family.

A few years earlier, I'd lost my own special little dog, Snoopy, in very tragic circumstances. Snoopy was a black, dachshund cross something or other, we never knew what, and he was my precious friend. I'd got him, as usual, from a rescue centre. He'd been in a pen with four boisterous six month old Springer Spaniel pups. It had been difficult for him to get my attention, smothered as he was in a moving swarm of excitement, but he'd finally managed. Every time he worked his way to the front and jumped up at the wall, eyes pleading, he'd be sent flying. The lady seemed surprised when I picked him out, but was pleased that her 'ugly duckling' had found a home. He wasn't ugly, not at all, just a little vertically challenged, and not in any way aristocratic. He had a long body and quite short legs, but to me he was perfect. He had the most adorable face and the biggest brown eyes. It was love at first sight for me.

Snoopy loved everyone, without exception, but he loved me the most. He'd follow me anywhere, even when I rode my Welsh Cob, Sky, across the nearby fields. Snoopy's little legs would go nineteen to the dozen as he managed to keep up with his giant four-legged friend. The most noticeable thing about him was that he was such a happy dog.

One day I was out walking with him when he got chased by some un-muzzled greyhounds. It was hardly a fair contest. Snoopy was petrified, as he might well be, with their giraffe-like legs speeding gaping rows of teeth towards him. All I could do was scream encouragement as he tore towards me, and run towards him. Maybe they thought his short legs made him a rabbit or hare? Thank goodness he reached me in time. I scooped him up into my arms, turning my back on the huge dogs, trusting that I didn't look anything like a rabbit! The owner protested, saying his dogs wouldn't have hurt mine, but with that size differential I couldn't have taken any chances.

Snoopy came everywhere with the family, including on holiday, where he always charmed everyone he met. He was such a little gentleman. I remember one farmer's wife whom we stayed with in Devon, complimenting him for his, 'Butiful jacket'. He certainly was the shiniest dog you'd ever seen. He also loved to swim in the farm's defunct swimming pool, never mind the fact that it was also full of indignant frogs. He loved our snappy little grey Lhasa Apaso, Tasha, who we had at the time, despite her grumpy nature, and she loved him. Peri was a member of our family too, back then. She was one of those really photogenic, pretty but scruffy dogs, with a whiskery face, and she and Snoopy were great pals. Snoopy used to lie across my shoulders when I relaxed, lying on the sofa, something like a cross between a parrot and a kitten. He'd climb up and settle down there for the evening. It was like wearing a heavy fox-fur collar.

Sadly, we only had Snoopy for three very short years.

I felt so awful when he died; so guilty. He had a habit of fetching stones, and he seemed quite sensible about it. He would even dive under fast flowing water and come up with a pebble in his mouth. I never thought anything of it. I didn't think it was dangerous, but tragically, I was wrong. One day Snoopy swallowed a stone. We didn't know he'd done it. It was a stone that had sharp edges. He showed no ill-effects during that day, but by morning he was in pain and moaning. I rushed him to the vet and they took him straight into surgery. I remember passing him to the nurse, and him looking back at me anxiously.

"It'll be alright," I promised him through the tears. We'd never spent a day apart. He was only three years old and had all his life in front of him.

Later that evening the vet called to say that he had removed a stone from Snoopy's intestines, and although it had done quite a bit of damage he had come round and would be fine. I could collect him in the morning. I was so happy! I couldn't wait. I hardly slept that night, but in the morning I phoned the vets as they'd requested, to make sure he was well enough to be collected. The receptionist said that the vet wanted to speak to me, and right away I knew something was wrong.

"I'm so sorry," he said, and my heart lurched. "I'm afraid your dog took a turn for the worse, and despite trying everything to save him, he died at midnight. I'm afraid the stone must have done more damage than we had thought."

My world shattered. My little dog had been snatched away. I'd been so excited at the thought of collecting him, so relieved that he was going to be alright, and now, suddenly, I'd never see him again. It was a terrible shock, especially as I'd already been told he'd recovered. They had said he was fine. It must have been my fault. I felt as if I'd abandoned him. I told myself, foolishly I know, that if only I'd been with him, things would have been different. I thought he must have given up because I wasn't there. If I'd been there I would have given him the will to live. Of course it wasn't true. He'd been sedated and wouldn't have known I was there, but I blamed myself nevertheless. If only I'd realized sooner that he was hurt. *If only*. They have to be the worst words to be left with.

What really haunted me, and still does even now, was that I'd heard him give a whine or two in the night, but had dismissed it as his usual behaviour with Tasha or Peri. Even though they'd been spayed, he was entire, and would still respond to them every now and then. He would whine at his inability to do what nature was telling him to do. God help me, I'd even called out to him to be quiet in the middle of the night and he'd obediently quietened down. Then in the morning, I'd realized my little dog was in great pain. That was what was destroying me. I'd scolded him when he needed me. What must he have thought? It really didn't bear thinking about. Of course I would have done anything for my dog had I realized something was wrong, as Tony kept telling me. All the same, that night will always live with me, and I'll always wish I could turn back the clock and change things.

I was so distraught at the time that I rode Sky down to the empty fields and called out for Snoopy to come home. Everywhere seemed so empty without his little black shape bombing around, and like any bereaved person, my dearest wish was to know where he was, and if he was all right. I thought I'd never get over the loss of him.

At that point I'd thought *no more*. We'd still have our family dogs, but never again would I have a dog that felt so much like a soul mate. It hurt too much. I meant it too, and for several years that was the way it was. We lost Tasha a couple of years later, after she went blind at age twelve, and we had a new small, black dog, called Nyssa, who looked a lot like Snoopy. She became the matriarch, always there to sort out any squabbles between our dogs. She was lovely, but she wasn't a dog especially for me. I didn't want one who was. It was too hard. I was certainly a dog lover, but I thought I was never going to want another dog of my own.

But that was before I met a certain black puppy, who had been found on the beach in Great Yarmouth, almost dead from scalds, and from swallowing sea water.

CHAPTER 4

Coming Home

The puppy was mystified. Every human she'd ever known since the day she was born had seemed to be evil, and yet when she woke up the next morning, despite the fact that she felt a bit trapped by the tubes that were attached to her, and the cage that held her, the voice she could hear softly humming sounded so gentle. She was drawn to the sound of a human voice for the first time in her life. So much so that she wondered, could this be a kind person? Everywhere in the room was white and clean, even the clothes the woman wore. It was so different from anything the pup had ever seen before.

Maggie Jones had worked for the Animal Rescue Centre in Yarmouth for twenty years. She'd seen cruel things during her time that would have made a lesser person run for the hills, but she had gritted her teeth and carried on. She had to, because her love for the animals was so strong, it just wouldn't let her walk away. She lived alone in a tiny terraced house in the town with no garden, which was probably just as well, otherwise she'd have been constantly taking waifs and strays home with her.

Maggie had never been married, never had children, and had saved all her energy for helping dogs such as this one. Her greatest pleasure in life came from homing one of the lost dogs with a loving new family and seeing them blossom and gain confidence in their new homes.

She didn't stop humming as she spotted slight movement out of the corner of her eye. The puppy had come round. She'd sensed a huge amount of fear in this young dog. Despite her weakness, when Maggie had picked her up from the damp sand, the pup had still struggled to get away at first. Maggie knew you couldn't rush these things. You couldn't force trust on a dog. All the same she felt there was something special about the black pup. All her charges were special to her of course, but there was something she couldn't put her finger on that made her think that this animal had something special to do in its life. It had an air of importance around it. She laughed at her own thoughts, *You're goin' barmy girl!*

She carried on humming to herself as she wiped down the counters, slowly but surely approaching the cage, but always keeping her back to it. She'd discovered that when a dog was very scared, it paid to approach it backwards. It was something to do with energy she thought. Humans project a lot of aggressive energy with the front of their bodies sometimes, as well as strong scent, whereas their backs were more neutral, less threatening. At last she felt the wire at her back and knew she'd be within scent of the puppy. She paused there, staying relaxed, still humming in a monotonous sort of way, and pressed herself back, so that the pup's inquisitive nose could utilize its incredible sense of smell and get used to her scent, without too much fear.

The pup was intrigued by what she could smell on the back of the woman's overall. Dogs, cats, strange chemical smells, cotton, shampoo from her hair and the sweet soapy smell of lavender. She didn't perceive any threat and the woman kept still, the soothing noise still coming from her. The puppy sensed the woman's energy too. Calm, friendly and no anxiety at all. After a few minutes the woman slowly turned around, but she made no attempt to look at the puppy. She kept her head low and slowly reached up to unlatch the cage door. The puppy tensed, but felt confident enough to stay where she was. She felt much better. Her wounds didn't hurt so much, and somehow she knew this human was responsible for helping her.

Maggie opened the door, showing trust in the puppy to not to try and jump out. The pup whimpered a bit as her slight movement flexed the tender skin on her chest.

"Oh poor baby," said Maggie, quietly, her sympathy at the wounds overcoming her knowledge that she had to be strong and keep her energy re-assuring. Emotional response made your energy weak to a dog's senses, she knew, and this poor little thing needed strong leadership to make her feel safe. Feeling sorry for the dog wouldn't help her feel better. Sure enough the pup reacted to Maggie's tension by pulling back slightly, but she couldn't get far away, so she just quivered at the back of the cage. Maggie felt inside her pocket for the soothing ointment-covered tissues she kept there ready. Moving very slowly she reached in and dabbed the delicate skin of the drained abscesses on the pup's chest.

"I'd like to meet whoever did this to you," Maggie muttered in a sing-song voice, not wanting the pup to sense any tension in her. "I'd like to break their necks, I would, oh yes I would."

The pup felt she should try and escape and she pulled back further in alarm as the tissue touched her, but then, she felt pure bliss as the ointment cooled the still slightly burning skin, and she moaned in pleasure. The sound surprised her as she'd never heard herself do that before. She looked so comically surprised that the woman laughed. This made the pup even more amazed. She'd never heard a laugh like it. The only laughter she'd ever heard had been the drunken cackling of the other woman and the man she'd lived with, and that had never signified anything pleasant. But this woman's laugh was different. It made the pup's tongue loll, and the corners of her mouth wrinkle upwards.

As the weeks passed by and turned from one to three, the pup, now 13 weeks old, was ready to be re-homed. Her abscesses were gone, but she was scarred for life. No fur would ever grow where the scalding water had burned it off. She would always carry the soft pink patches of baldness on her chest and the upper part of her right front leg. Maggie sighed. It wasn't fair. She was going to have trouble finding the right home for this little girl, she just knew it. She named the puppy Chloe, hoping that the cute-sounding, feminine name would attract people to her, make her sound prettier, and maybe they wouldn't notice the scars. But it didn't seem to work. People were so afraid of what others would think of them. They said they'd be ashamed to walk the puppy down the street, in case people thought they were the ones who had done the damage to her.

Finally, one day in September, a young couple agreed to take the puppy. They were very sweet people, but Maggie had misgivings. This puppy needed huge sensitivity, and these two weren't very experienced. She would be their first dog together as they were only recently married. But they seemed kind and gentle, and they might be the pup's only chance, so she had no choice really. Even so, Maggie had a tear in her eye as they carried Chloe off to their car. The pup had not wanted to go to them, hiding behind Maggie's legs. The pup whined as she was put in the car, and her eyes stared back beseechingly at Maggie, as if to say, *You're the only friend I've ever had. These are not the right people!*

The very next day Maggie's fears were realized as the couple brought Chloe back, arriving as Maggie was just opening up.

"Sorry," said the husband, handing the puppy over, "But this dog is completely crazy. She had the runs all night, howled all night, and then in the morning we found that she'd torn down and destroyed our living room curtains. You'll have to take her back. She's too much for us to handle."

Maggie cuddled the dog in her arms. In truth she was pleased to see her, but she wanted the pup to have a real life, not live the whole of it in kennels.

"Oh dear," she mouthed in the pup's ear, "What are we going to do with you?"

The pup was relieved to be home. She was even more relieved to see the woman, Maggie. The couple had been nice to her at first, but she was too scared to let either of them get too close, and had spent the day hiding behind the sofa. They'd tried to tempt her out with delicious smelling treats, but in her anxiety, she didn't feel all that hungry. But then, when it got dark, and they went to bed, she'd wolfed the treats down all at once. As the night wore on and the shadows deepened, she became terrified. She had cried and cried, but they hadn't taken any notice.

To the pup, every dark corner held a possibility that the 'man' was hiding there, waiting to throw the water that burned on her again. Eventually the rich treats and her nerves had got the better of her bowels and she'd tried to get outside, but couldn't find a way. She'd torn down the curtains in her attempt to get to the open quarter-light window, but she couldn't reach it. She didn't want to mess indoors, but she had no choice. Finally she curled up exhausted on the ravaged curtains on the window ledge and waited for the dawn. Of course when the couple came down in the morning, they were furious. The man had scooped the pup up before she could run and shoved her back in the car. The trip to the kennels took place in stony silence. The pup was glad to be back in her cage, where she felt safe. She never wanted to leave home again.

Maggie was in two minds, disappointed that Chloe hadn't found a home, and yet happy to have her to cuddle again. She was the only puppy in the kennels at that time, and so she was top of the list, attention-wise. Later that day the phone rang, and a female voice asked if the kennels had any puppies wanting a home. Maggie found herself almost talking the woman out of it, explaining about the scars and that most people were put off by them, explaining that the pup was proving difficult to home and had been returned once as 'crazy', but bizarrely nothing seemed to do the trick. The woman said, "I want her."

The pup heard Maggie's tone of voice and knew she was being talked about. Someone was coming to take her. She thought she should be scared, but a warm glow settled over her. She should have been concerned at who was coming to take her from her 'home', but she wasn't. She didn't understand it at all, but as dogs do, she just accepted the feeling. Her intuition was in full working order. This was the life she was destined for. She felt a little fizz of anticipation. It was happening. What was 'meant to be' was happening.

A few hours later, Maggie took Chloe from her cage and carried her out to the van. Her heart was sinking. She had to let the puppy go at some point, but supposing these people turned out to be wrong? Maggie settled the pup into the cage in the back of the van and set off. The only thing that kept her hopes up was the fact that Chloe seemed very calm, in fact oddly so. The woman who'd phoned was relatively new to the area and the kennels were tricky to find, so she and Maggie had made an arrangement to meet at a roundabout on an industrial estate. It was on Maggie's way home, so not too far out of her way, but absurdly, Maggie felt a bit like a spy as she waited at the rendezvous point. Chloe was very quiet. She sat in the cage in the back of the van, not stressing, and not whining, which was a bit weird. The pup didn't feel excitement exactly, just a sense of 'rightness' unfolding. She knew, just somehow knew, that the 'someone' who was coming to take her, was someone that was *meant* to take her. Her nose and paws tingled with the quiet knowledge that everything was as it should be, and was going to be alright. She waited.

CHAPTER 5

Do I Know You?

As I put the phone down, Tony walked into the room, a questioning look on his face.

"Yes," I answered his unspoken question, "They have one – just one. Poor little thing, she's been through a really bad time. She's scarred and people don't want her because they're ashamed to walk down the street with her."

I didn't mention that the pup had been returned to the kennels once as 'crazy' because I didn't want to put him off. I felt a really deep sense that this was inevitable, that we were meant to have this dog no matter what her problems were. It was as if I had no choice in the matter but was just led to the meeting. This dog was going to be something special, I thought, but at that point I had no idea just how special she was going to be.

It seemed a bit odd, picking up a puppy on road on a round-about, but as we approached I could see why Maggie had chosen it. At that time of day the industrial estate was pretty much deserted and it was very easy to find. My heart started beating a little faster as we moved towards the meeting. I could see a white van parked there as we pulled up, and a lady, I assumed to be Maggie, was standing in front of it. Tony parked the car and we got out. I still had a strange, unattached and yet electric feeling, as if I was merely a passenger in my own body.

After a brief greeting, Maggie said, "I've told you everything about this puppy. She really does need a sensitive owner, but she has so much to give. All I ask is, please, once you've met her, think about it, be honest, and only take her if you really want her. It's not good for her at all to be constantly unsettled. When you meet her, please remember that she won't be friendly at first. She doesn't trust anyone – she's had no reason to. So don't be put off when she acts scared of you. Don't take it personally."

"OK," was all I could say at that moment. I was smiling inside though, thinking, *if we really want her? Of course we really want her!* This was a strange thing to think, bearing in mind that we hadn't even clapped eyes on the puppy at that point.

Then looking as if she was thinking, *Well that's it. I can't put if off any longer,* Maggie turned and went to the back of the van, and we heard her open the doors and delve inside. We could hear her talking to the puppy as she got her out of the cage. "Be good now. Don't be scared. It puts people off when you cower away from them. They'll be nice to you. I'm sure they will. They won't mind a bit of settling in mess. Whatever you do, don't bark at them."

She was obviously saying these things loudly, quite deliberately, still trying to prepare us for how she expected the pup to react to us. Because of that I fully expected to see her dragging an unwilling dog behind her to the front of the van, but it didn't happen like that. As she walked up the side of the van, a beautiful, young black dog followed her, head up, tail up. The puppy looked very calm – way too calm for a young puppy, more like a mature dog. Maggie's face said it all, as she glanced down disbelievingly at the unexpected transformation at her side. She was obviously amazed too.

"This is Chloe," Maggie announced as if she didn't quite believe that it was, as she brought the dog forward. The pup and I locked eyes, and then, with no excitement or fuss at all, she left Maggie's side, and pulling the lead out to its full length, she walked to me, then turned around and sat down beside me, her shoulder against my leg. I was breathless. I felt tears welling in my eyes, and I could see them in Maggie's too. "Well," I said, smiling, "that seems to be that."

Maggie looked a little upset as she handed me the lead and patted Chloe's head, telling her, "You be a good girl, now. I'll miss you." Then she turned and got back in her van. "Take care of her," she called out in parting, "She deserves it." There was a flash of white handkerchief and then with a brief wave she started her van, turned it around and drove off.

What a remarkable, incredibly strong woman, I thought, *to be able to help these animals and then let them go.* People who have the strength to witness cruelty and then calmly act on it have always had my admiration. I knew I wouldn't be capable of doing it.

The pup still sat, motionless at my side, looking straight ahead. As Maggie walked away I'd wondered if Chloe would start after her, or whimper, but she never moved or made a sound. I looked at Tony, and we both grinned. I bent down and picked up my dog, because without any doubt I knew at this moment, that she was *my* dog. She was mine and I was hers. We got in the car, and with Chloe on my lap we drove home.

I gently fingered the soft, delicate, velvety skin of her hairless patches. "Poor baby," I murmured. She looked up and me, her eyes soft and warm. She seemed to appreciate my sympathy. She sighed like someone who had reached home after a long, long journey, then flopped down across my knees and fell fast asleep.

As we drove along, and we talked about it, we knew that Chloe wasn't her right name. It was too fragile sounding. She was majestic, not just pretty like that name, and if she was ever to escape the trauma that had caused her scars, she would need a strong sounding name that reflected balance and power. She needed a title that gave off the right positive energy to help her self-esteem and healing. We'd developed a habit of naming our recent dogs after Dr Who assistants, already having Nyssa and Peri, and there was one other name we'd never used that was perfectly right for this dog. Her name was Ace.

For the first few days Ace didn't want to leave my side. It wasn't easy at times, but she never misbehaved at all, just sat there. We introduced her successfully to our other two dogs, and only separated them at night, to start with, just in case there were any arguments. When people came to visit, they couldn't believe that Ace was just a puppy. At thirteen weeks old, she behaved more like a fat, elderly, Labrador than a vibrant young dog. It was nice that she felt so close to me, and so comfortable with me, but her behaviour wasn't right for a young puppy. She should have been full of playfulness and getting into mischief, not acting like a service dog, but I was sure that normality would come in time.

Despite her angelic behaviour when she was with me, we did have one mishap. The first night that I left her alone downstairs (we didn't want to start off with her being allowed in our bedroom, and get 'spoilt'), although we didn't hear much from her, by morning she'd bitten and clawed her way through a solid wooden door. It seemed that she felt safe with me, but frantic without me. All that stopped once we were secure enough to let her sleep with the other dogs for company. Eventually Ace started to relax with her family and adopt more puppy-like behavior. As if sensing her need to be shown how to play and socialize, Nyssa became Ace's surrogate mother. She would let the puppy play with her like she was a giant soft toy, play fighting, being rolled around, and as Ace got bigger, Nyssa had no objections to being dragged around the floor by one of her legs. Enough was enough though, and suddenly after a couple of months Nyssa said, no more, you're too big now, and the rough and tumble stopped. I have rarely come across a dog with such a good nature as Nyssa. There really wasn't an ounce of malice in her little body.

One morning I took Ace shopping with me, instead of leaving her at home with the other dogs. They all got on very well by then, but I still wasn't ready to leave the 'pack' without their leader, (me), just in case. I only had one shop to go in, so I took Ace to the railing outside and tied her lead to it. I would have been able to see her all the time while I was in the small shop, and she'd be able to see me. But as I went though the door I glanced back at her, and her face just broke my heart. I'd never seen a dog look as bleak before, I thought. Then I remembered, it was the exact look Snoopy had on his face as I'd handed him to the vet that day. I couldn't do it, *not again* I thought.

That was the moment a very strange thought came into my mind. I wondered, just for a moment, could Ace actually *be* Snoopy? I'd heard about the theory of reincarnation of course, but had never heard it applied to dogs. It did seem very odd, the way she seemed to know me and trust me, right from the very first second, and the way she left her only friend, Maggie, quite willingly, to come and sit at my side. Mind you, she didn't really trust Tony at first. She would obey him, but he couldn't get hold of her or restrain her in any way, without her panicking, so surely I must be wrong, because Snoopy had trusted him completely. It was the same thing with our son, Phillip. Why would she remember me and not Tony, or our son? It seemed silly, so I dismissed the idea.

This fear of hers wasn't Tony's or Phillip's fault. By now, they were totally besotted with Ace, and wanted her to trust them more than anything, but they didn't force her, knowing, hoping, that in time she would come to trust them herself. She was one of those dogs with an indefinable, noble, quality that drew nice people to her.

CHAPTER 6

Gaining Confidence

When she saw her new owner for the first time, the puppy was overcome with a feeling of security. For the first time in her short life, that one thing she'd always longed for was hers. She felt safe. She felt at peace. It seemed perfectly natural that she should just go and sit next to this person. She didn't remotely understand why this person made her feel so safe, but as dogs do, she lived in the moment. The fact that she did feel safe was all that mattered. The energy coming from her new owner was familiar in some way, and flowed over her like a gentle caress. She didn't question it.

She loved her new home; lovely warm beds, a nice pack, plenty of food, and a wonderful field to run around in. When people came to visit, she was always on her best behaviour, keeping very quiet and sitting in the energy of her owner. The new dogs in her pack were very nice too, and everything looked rosy.

When she was left alone that first night though, she didn't feel safe at all. Panic overtook her and she switched it off by digging and biting at the barrier between herself and the woman she felt safe with. After a while though, the panic subsided, because the woman always came back in the morning. The puppy began to relax, understanding that the separation was only temporary. A few days later she was allowed to sleep with the other two dogs and that helped. After a quick sniff of introduction they had seemed to accept her into their pack. The three of them snuggled down warmly together, and for the pup it was like being with her own family – something she had only ever experienced for a short time before.

When she was taken to the town in the car, and the woman had almost left her outside the shop, tied to a railing, the pup felt a sense of abandonment creeping over her, and her spirit almost tore, but then the woman didn't leave her after all.

She came back, untying the lead and saying, "I'm sorry Ace, I won't leave you again." The pup didn't understand the words but she understood that she wasn't going to be left, and that was OK.

She often found herself looking at the man and the boy, and slowly realizing that they weren't people to be afraid of. This man wasn't like the other man, he didn't shout or get angry, but still, she didn't want him to trap her. If he tried to hold her, she'd have a panic attack and whimper and struggle. Sometimes, she looked at him and felt that she had trusted him before, but it was not enough to make her relax totally with him. She never tried to get on the couch next to him, preferring to stay by the woman's side. The trauma she'd been through had broken something inside her soul. But she knew that one day she'd like to trust again, and that one day she would.

One of her favourite times with the woman was when she would gently stroke the bald areas of skin that were the Ace's lifelong legacy from the attack, cooing, "Poor puppy, poor puppy." Instead of shying away from the scars in embarrassment, the woman would show them to people, saying, "Look what they did to her." The person she was showing them to would be very sympathetic. It made the dog feel almost proud of her battle-scars, and made her feel more secure that nothing like that would ever be allowed to happen to her again.

Daytimes were fun, as the dogs got to run around the field. Gradually, Ace started to learn to play, to run and jump in the long grass, like a normal puppy. The field was laden with exciting smells. Rabbits, stoats, weasels and foxes had roamed there at night, and their scents hung in the droplets of dew on the grass and in the thick field maple and hawthorn hedgerow. There was a ditch at the bottom of the field and the grassy slopes held interesting temporary lakes of water after wet weather. There were three horses and nine sheep in the field too, but the pup understood immediately that they were part of the pack, owned by the pack leaders, and not to be chased. It was funny how she just knew, but she didn't question it. It just was.

Each morning she'd race around the field, whatever the weather, following the scents, reveling in her freedom, growing stronger. Sometimes she'd come across an unusual smell which would intrigue her irresistibly, and one day, this led her into danger. There was a hole in the ground, just a small one, and the soil around the hole was spongy and strange. Normally, such a hole would smell of mice, rats or voles, but this one was different. At first she circled it, wary and wondering what kind of creature could live there. It was like nothing she'd ever smelled before.

Curiosity overcoming caution, she stuck her nose into the hole, wondering what was down there. For a while there was nothing, and then suddenly she felt an excruciating pain in the soft tissue of her nose, and she leapt back. Small, yellow and black, stripy creatures whirled out of the hole and spun around her head. One wasp landed on her muzzle, and the pup screeched as it stung her again. Memories of the attack with the burning water rose in her mind, and she froze in fear, not knowing what to do. She'd felt so safe and now she was terrified all over again. Her legs wouldn't move, and the flying creatures closed in around her, wriggling through her fur, trying to penetrate her skin. One landed on the soft, scarred skin of her chest, where there was no protection, and she leapt off the ground, yelping.

Her yelp ended with a surprised squeak, as suddenly the pup was snatched up into the air and whirled away. The woman had picked her up and was running with her in her arms. The buzzing, angry creatures didn't give up right away though, and as the pup bounced along, being carried, she could hear the woman's cries as the nasty beasts stung her on her arms. The woman didn't give up either, despite being stung, and she shielded the pup as she ran. Eventually the yellow and black creatures lost their fury and gave up, disappearing as woman and dog neared the house. The woman rained kisses on the pup's swollen bites. She carried her indoors and put soothing, pungent liquid on them, and the stinging went away immediately.

The pup was amazed. She had felt safe with the woman before, but didn't know why she had. Now the pup understood that this human would even risk her own life to keep her safe. The knowledge was overwhelming. Not since her own mother had gone had the little dog felt a connection so strong. The pup knew that she would do the same if the woman ever needed defending. Yes, she would grow up big and strong and be the woman's defender. That was the job she had been born to do. Ace even knew that should that terrible 'man' come after her one day, she would be a guard before she would be a coward in his presence.

Her time would come when she'd need to be courageous, and she'd be ready. Two years passed very slowly to Ace. She grew stronger in mind and body and more confident by the day. She was a big dog by then and had a gorgeous, glossy, black coat, with swirls and curls here and there. She was black like a Labrador, but her muzzle and ears were pure German Shepherd. Her new teeth were a startling white, and fearsome. She was no longer a puppy, but 'Puppy' was still her nickname, and would be until the day she died. She became a wonderful guard dog, and knew it would have taken a very brave burglar to face her.

She had learned to chase rabbits for fun. But if ever she actually caught one, it was only because they were sick or injured. Sometimes if the woman came across a dying rabbit, horrifically blind from myxamatosis, that evil, man-made disease, its eyes swelled shut, or one badly injured by a fox or car, she would call Ace, because the dog instinctively knew how to kill them quickly and mercifully and that truly was the quickest way to put the rabbit out of its misery. One quick bite through their spine at the back of their neck, and death was instantaneous.

Another milestone that was to change things finally happened one evening. It had been a tiring day, as the family had been for a long walk on the beach. It wasn't the one that Ace was found on, but the salty smells and the sand reminded her of it. She still marveled at all the water, but this time was very different to the first visit. She knew better than to drink any of it. She just played in the surf as it ran back and forth tickling her toes, sniffed exciting scraps of dead fish left among the pebbles, and dared the crabs in rock pools to snip at her nose. On the sandy dunes she smelled rabbits and foxes, their 'scenty' traces telling her powerful, doggy nose the complete story of what had gone on there overnight. There was a ball to chase, and the three dogs raced to reach it first. Each of the dogs was given an ice-cream before they left, which Ace adored. By the time they got home they were exhausted.

Later, after food and water, Ace found her gaze drawn again and again to the man, where he sat on the sofa. He often called to her, inviting her to sit with him, but although she obeyed by going as far as his feet, she still couldn't bear to put herself in a vulnerable position with him. He was a quiet, gentle man, not prone to violent outbursts of temper, but it was difficult for her to allow herself to become vulnerable to him. But that evening, something had changed. She was starting to understand his energy. Shady memories of knowing his energy from some time before kept coming over her. She felt the start of a little joy in her heart, although she didn't understand it. What she *did* know was that now was the time.

The couple noticed that she kept looking at the man in a strange way, and were obviously puzzled by it. Suddenly Ace stood up, her eyes still on the man. She felt a strong pull, and step by step, she slowly walked over to him. He seemed to deliberately be avoiding eye contact with her. Ace gave a soft whine. This time she wanted to make eye contact. The man turned his eyes to hers, and brown on brown, they linked.

Ace sighed deeply. She had an overwhelming sense that everything was going to be alright from now on for the whole of her life. She stepped up onto the sofa with her front feet and then hopped the back ones up to join them. She carefully picked her way onto his lap, and lay down, front legs one side, hind legs the other, belly across his legs. The man stroked her head. Ace sighed again and went to sleep right where she was.

From that moment things were different in the pack. They were united and bonded together in a way she had thought she'd never know. As Ace became confident enough to trust the son too, she'd felt secure enough to greet strangers, once her pack had introduced them as friends.

Her heart was so full of joy that she wondered when she would be called upon to give something back. One day that moment came, the moment she'd been waiting for, the day when she was to save the woman's life.

CHAPTER 7

Fulfilling Contracts

On the day when Ace got attacked by a nest full of disturbed wasps we were all walking around the field, and Ace seemed intrigued by something she could smell in the long grass. She was nose down, tail up, wagging her whole body furiously, as she investigated. I was watching all three dogs, wondering at the different way they all 'hunted'. Peri would take vast sweeping circles, covering the whole field time and time again. Nyssa, a much slower dog, would creep along, hoping to surprise something, and then pounce. Ace would do a combination of both, sweeping for scents and then becoming stealthy when she found one.

Spotting her still with her nose down I assumed it was one of the usual animal smells, so I was shocked when she suddenly cried out and jumped back. An angry, buzzing cloud poured out of the hole in the ground. She'd stuck her nose into a wasp's nest. I was twenty yards from her and Tony was at the other end of the field. Ace started yelping, and seemed rooted to the spot, even though I called her name. I ran towards her, my heart thudding. Who knew what damage a wasp swarm could do to her.

I was breathless by the time I reached her, and she'd yelped twice more by then. Frantically, I scooped her up into my arms and ran towards the house. I could see Tony was running up the field, but there was little he could do. I tried to shield Ace, wrapping her in my arms and the furious wasps stuck their little barbs into me wherever they could find bare skin. It didn't matter – I wasn't going to let Ace get stung anymore. I wasn't allergic to wasp stings, so it was just a question of pain. She'd been through enough of that in her life already, and I also found a stray thought enter my mind as I ducked and dived my way to the house and safety. *This time, I have the power to save you.*

By then I'd reached the garden, and the wasps pretty much gave up. Just one or two persisted, and I swatted them away easily. Once inside the house I put Ace down on the floor, and by the time Tony arrived to see if we were all right, I was bathing both of our stings with vinegar, knowing that the wasp stings were alkaline and the acid in the vinegar would counteract it. As if by magic, the pain went away.

Ace licked my hand, knowing I'd been the one to help her. Our eyes locked, and something new passed between us. It was something I can't explain, like the universe giving a twitch. Something deep and meaningful was taking place, a shift in both our perceptions.

It was a few nights later that Tony, who was sitting watching television, said quietly, "Jen, look at her." I looked, and Ace was standing right in front of Tony where he sat on the sofa, staring hard at him, meeting his eyes, something she'd never done before. Another change was taking place. I held my breath. Ace looked away from him, and then looked back, as if something was drawing her eyes irresistibly. The other two dogs seemed frozen in place where they lay. You could have heard a pin drop in the room as Ace carefully placed one paw and then another on the sofa right next to him. I willed her on, silently. She jumped the rest of the way up, lay down across Tony's legs, sighed, and went to sleep. Tony and I locked eyes across the sleeping dog, total joy radiating between us. From that day on, Ace trusted Tony implicitly.

She started to become more and more trusting after that, becoming very loving with Phillip, even welcoming strangers into our house, so long as *we* did (she would still have been a scourge to any unauthorized visitors). She would peer at strangers as they entered the house. I would put an arm around their shoulders and say, "This is a friend, Puppy." From that moment she treated them all like members of the family.

The only time I ever had a problem was when a young lad came to collect some waste wood from us. He was a nice lad and Ace was fine with him at first, but later she was close by, watching, as he emerged from our shed into the light. As he turned, his hair was lit from behind, standing up, spiky. Ace suddenly went totally bonkers. She barked at him aggressively and I really think she might have attacked him if I hadn't grabbed her and dragged her inside. It only ever happened that once, and it was totally out of character. I apologized to the lad, and at the time I thought I'd never know why she did it.

Together with our horses, we also had pet sheep in our field. Horses destroy good grazing eventually, because they're such selective and fussy eaters, and the dreaded yellow weed, ragwort, could even kill them in time. If we'd just had horses they would have also left any grass soured by their droppings, and soon the field would have been dotted with rank patches, where only yellow grass and nettles would grow. Also, horse parasites would have multiplied out of control. Sheep eat a lot of weeds, even ragwort, with impunity, and horses will graze over sheep's droppings quite happily. By having a balance of sheep and horses on the land it would stay sweet and green. In the early summer we would fence off a large portion of the field and have it cut for hay. I loved the process. It was always a worry whether the hay would dry and stay fresh or get rained into nasty moldy clumps, but if it was a successful crop, we loved watching as the bales slid off the back of the baler.

The first spring we were there with our own land, we went to the local livestock market. There we found trailers full of orphan lambs whose mothers had died or had rejected them. It was a pitiful sight, but we were glad we could help some of them. Of course, with us they had the added benefit of not ever being killed and eaten, as they would be our permanent grass-mowers.

We started off with three orphan lambs. We got a ram, Teddy, (so that we could breed a few more to keep the balance right) and two ewes, Rosie and Smudge. We bottle fed them all, and it was great fun. It could be a bit tiring feeding them regularly from bottles, but at least unlike human babies, they would sleep all night.

The next year the two ewes had lambs of their own, Rosie and Smudge each had a set of twins. One of Smudge's black twins was lifeless, and despite my eventually getting it to breathe by pumping its chest, Smudge rejected it, butting it away with her head when I tried to get her to sniff or lick it. I was afraid she would kill it, so I took it inside, wondering if it had any chance to survive.

When born, like human babies, lambs are covered with a filmy membrane, and if the mother sheep doesn't clean it off, it has to be washed off. It's a dodgy procedure because the lambs get very cold, very quickly, and whereas their mother's tongue would have dried them, a wash would make them even wetter. I was already calling this little baby ram, Sooty, as if by naming him I would ensure his survival. I walked into the kitchen with him wrapped in a big towel, unsure what to do. He was breathing well, but shivering. If I'd had an Aga, I could have popped him inside to warm up, but I didn't, so I had to think of another way. I could have rubbed him vigorously with the towel, but my amazing dog had other ideas. Ace had watched me as I stood holding the lamb, indecisive. Then she started licking his long, wet tail where it dangled from the towel. On impulse I put the open blanket on the floor and laid the lamb on it. Ace immediately went in and started licking. The lamb quickly started to rally as her warm tongue massaged it. By the time Ace had cleaned all the membrane off, Sooty was getting lively and trying to stand up. Trusting her completely, I left Ace to look after him and went to fetch a bottle of substitute sheep's milk.

My dog never failed to astound me. She'd always chased rabbits out in the field and seemed to know instinctively how to dispatch them, literally in a second, if they were sick or hurt. She never played with them, or had fun at their expense; just a quick snap and they were dead. And yet here was that same dog, still in possession of those killing teeth, diligently caring for a tiny, newborn lamb. In time I came to realize that this was a dog with compassion.

Our first baby boy lamb, saved at the market, Teddy, had grown into a massive two year old brute and had effortlessly sired his off-spring. His name, which had suited him when he was a cuddly baby, didn't really suit 200lbs of ram. It turned out, we discovered later, that bottle fed rams (and bulls) can get very disrespectful to their human keepers when they grow up. They don't see you as human, but think you're another ram (or bull). Teddy was probably just being playful when he charged, but it wasn't any fun for us. He would run as fast as he could, take off from about two yards away in a mighty leap, and crash his bony head into you at about thigh height. It was obviously dangerous, but we thought we could cope. He had no horns, and contrarily this made it even more difficult when he started charging us. If he'd had horns we'd have had something to grab hold of and use to control his head a bit, but his head was smooth and hornless, quite the battering ram. At first it was reasonably amusing dodging his attentions, but soon it took on a more sinister note.

One day I was home alone and as normal in the afternoon I took the dogs for a run around the field. I was coming back, the dogs sniffing around as usual all over the eight acres of the field, when I saw Teddy approaching me at a fair speed. I'd been silly, I hadn't brought a stick or crook, I was too far from the edge of the field to take cover, and I was pretty much helpless. I didn't know what to do. I held out my hands and shouted at him in the vain chance of fending him off, but it was hopeless, Teddy was deadly serious this time. The ram left the ground, as I knew he would, and cannoned into me at hip height. I went flying. He'd hit me with his total weight and caught me just right. I crashed to the ground, shouting in pain. I struggled to get up, feeling very vulnerable on the ground, but I couldn't do it quickly enough to save myself. Teddy had run off and then turned around, and was lining himself up for another charge and another collision. The real problem was that this time he was coming at me at head height, and unless I could get up I was in very big trouble. My leg wouldn't support me, and I looked helplessly at Teddy as he started his run. All I could think of doing was to try and get lower so that he wouldn't get my head, and to cover my face with my arms, but there was murder in that ram's eye and he lowered his head to match my line of sight.

I closed my eyes when he was a couple of feet away, turning my head away from him. There was nothing else I could do. I waited for the blow to strike, thinking, incredulously, as I imagine other people must always do in similar situations, *this is it – I'm dead.* But the anticipated blow never landed. I opened my eyes seconds later in disbelief, to see Ace there, grabbing at Teddy's ear. The last time I'd noticed her she'd been right over the other side of the field, taking no interest in us. But she'd managed somehow to get across the field and between us and she'd turned him. I hadn't even registered her coming to us. She ran around the ram in circles, nipping at his ear every time he paid me any more attention, instead turning his anger on her. Luckily she was more agile than I was and dodged his charges easily. I finally managed to struggle to my feet and began the long hobble up the field. I wasn't out of danger yet. But Ace knew that too, and she continued to circle Teddy, 'worrying him', keeping his attention on her, until I got as far as the gate and was safe. Then she left him to it, haring up the field, to receive my grateful thanks. When we looked at Teddy later (keeping him suitably restrained), she hadn't even scratched the skin of his ear, she'd been so accurate and careful with her nips.

The next day Tony somberly drew my attention to an article in the daily paper. A farmer in Yorkshire had been killed by a ram he'd bottle fed. The ram had hit him in the hip, knocked him down, and then charged again, hitting him in the head. The farmer had suffered a fractured skull and been dead when he was found. My God...if it hadn't been for Ace...I would have been dead too. Teddy had to go, we accepted that, but we couldn't have him killed. He was a healthy and rather magnificent specimen. Surely someone could give him a safe home. In the meantime we kept him on a tether in the small paddock, for safety's sake. Thank goodness that very soon a knowledgeable local lady said she'd have him. All he needed, she assured us, was a bigger flock. Once he has plenty of ewes, he'd be fine. She was right, and Teddy had a good life.

CHAPTER 8

From a Dog's Point of View

Ace was nose down, tail up and wagging, at the far end of the field, the day the ram attacked the woman. The grass was dry, long and yellowing, but it still held the most amazing scents. It had rained the night before and drops clung to the plants as the scent clung to the water droplets. Occasional thistles poked purple heads above the grass, and red moths perched on them, feeding. Ace put her head up and snuffed the air. A kaleidoscope of smells wafted on the breeze. It was intoxicating. She put her head down again to concentrate on the smells on the ground. Here and there urine, that acidic but irresistibly pungent aroma, permeated the foliage, with each animal's scent slightly different from the rest. There was the deep, dry, acrid and rich tang of fox, the grassy smell of rabbits, and the exciting muskiness of weasels and stoats.

Badgers had been there too, she could tell, and she found one fascinating spot where an unfortunate hedgehog had met its demise at the hands of one of the black and white creatures. Ace had occasionally picked up an errant hedgehog in her mouth, very carefully, to avoid injuring it and also because of the spines, but her owner had gently chastised her and returned them unharmed to the long grass, so now she left them alone. She had a lot of respect for badgers though, who seemingly could actually eat a hedgehog, despite those prickles. Further on, tufts of fluffy rabbit fur marked the spot where a barn owl had swooped silently out of the darkness and carried one off. The fields were busy at night. Rabbits were especially interesting, because the people perceived them to be cute, cuddly, gentle creatures, whereas Ace had learned that they could be very aggressive, especially the males. Their sharp, raking claws were quite capable of trying to disembowel an attacker as the rabbit brought its scrabbling back feet into play. The most dangerous creatures, apart from the badgers and foxes that Ace had come across, were the weasels and stoats. These small animals could kill a rabbit in the blink of an eye, and the smell they gave off when alarmed, was eye-watering. Ace had come to understand these various creatures, without her humans ever noticing the signs of any, bar the rabbits, who were so obvious in their large numbers. It seemed the people had very little idea of the variety of the fauna that lived and died on their land.

Last summer the most amazing event, in Ace's eyes anyway, had happened. Tractors had come into the field and scythed down the long grass. The heaps of drying grass had been laid neatly into rows and left to dry in the sun. That evening, when the dogs had been let out, the field seemed entirely empty of animals. But then, when they'd been allowed out a few days later as the rapidly yellowing grass rows were turned, mice had poured from the hay as it was twitched over, streaming across the short grass and finding new hiding places. A few days later the grass was moved again, lifted up by a big machine. The machine spat the grass out again at the back, tied up in a square parcel. Mice and voles and rabbits fled around the field, closely chased by the dogs and the odd kestrel. There were so many targets to choose from, that all the dogs' potential victims escaped in the chaos, diving into the safety of the hedge.

The day the ram attacked, the following summer, the grass had been left to grow long and was going to seed. Wild flowers had sprouted. There were primroses, mulleins, daisies, buttercups, rosebay willow herbs and meadowsweet and mares-tails near the ditches. Ace didn't know their names, but she recognized them all by their scents. The hedgerows flickered as flocks of long tailed tits and redstarts passed through.

Ace was engrossed in the smells, sights and sounds of the

wildlife, but her ears were always open to her mistress, so she immediately heard her sharp cry of fear. That alone might not have galvanized her, but at the same time she also felt a rush of distressed energy. It poured across the field like water and hit her. She looked across the field, her doggy vision showing her little more than silhouettes at that distance, but the tone of the cry and the quality of the energy pulse, made her immediately abandon the wonderful scents she'd been investigating. She set off at a flat-out run across the bottom of the field towards the woman and the ram, her heartbeat racing as fast as she was. The old timid puppy in her would have been terrified at actually running towards danger, but Ace was overwhelmed with a sense of purpose, that was stronger than any fear. She hardly felt her paws touch the ground as she flew along.

As she got nearer, within seconds, Ace was assessing the situation ahead of her. The woman was on the ground, clutching at her hip, and trying to struggle to her feet, her arms held out towards the ram, which had backed off and was looking at her, red-eyed and beady. Ace immediately recognized it as being an animal in the 'red zone'. No amount of shouting or barking, or threats could penetrate the brain of an animal in this state. The woman was shouting, naturally, her voice full of fear. The sound tore something in Ace, she simply couldn't stand it.

Dilemma almost made her hesitate though. After all, she had never, ever, let a thought of touching a sheep aggressively enter her head before. The sheep belonged to the woman, and she accepted that totally. But, now the ram was getting ready for another charge. He revved himself up and thundered towards the figure on the ground, and there was no more time for doubts. The woman cried out again and threw up her arms to defend her head. Breathless, Ace leapt into the small space that separated them. As she landed, she snatched at the ram's ear, and using just enough of a grip to make him heed, without breaking the skin. The ram spun round and Ace turned with him. Once he was facing away from the woman, she released his ear, but his rage took over and he started another charge towards the woman. Ace pinched his ear again, and again, spinning out of reach of his powerful head when he turned his anger towards her.

The woman had managed to get to her feet by then and start limping, painfully, up the field, towards the gate and safety. But Ace daren't leave the ram, and so they circled, round and round, the dog baiting the ram until she saw the woman going safely through the gate and closing it behind her. Then she let go of the ear and ran to the gate herself, squeezing underneath, well-ahead of the outraged ram.

Ace was proud of herself, especially that evening when the woman recounted the tale of her bravery to the man. She was given treats and praised all evening. The dog felt that she'd done what she'd been born for, and her self-confidence grew in response to it. At night she had amazing dreams of places she had never seen. Her lips snarled and smiled in her sleep, and she whimpered in excitement as the smell and taste of deer filled her nose and mouth, even though she'd never seen such an animal. Her legs twitched as she galloped in the footsteps of a white horse, knowing that she had a very important job to do, protecting the small human who rode the horse. When she woke she never remembered the dreams, but she felt she was right where she was meant to be, doing what she was meant to do, and this thought filled her with a sense of fulfillment.

It was only weeks later, that the wheel turned again in the dog's and the woman's entwined lives. Ace was out walking with her whole pack, along the bank of a fast-moving body of water. The wind was blowing as it often did across the flat lands where they lived. The sun peeked between scudding clouds, and the water alternately sparkled with life and brooded with shadowy, green, roiling depths. Ace foraged happily along the hedgerow, smelling the daily 'nosepaper' of the animals that lived there, and the traces and messages of their daily lives. Life was good.

She crept under the hedge, following a particularly unusual smell, and was just pushing her way back onto the path when suddenly she came face to face with the creature that had created the scent. A three-foot long, skinny animal that slithered away, rather than running, as it had no legs. All these things ran through Ace's mind as she took one, two steps back to assess the possible danger from this bizarre creature. The grass snake opened his mouth wide, and an evil-looking forked tongue poked out, waggling around in the air. As the tongue waved at Ace, the creature reared up, its whole body stiffening into a curved arch, and poked its flat head towards her. What on earth was this bizarre creature? It was too much for Ace to comprehend, and she leapt backwards without thinking where she was going. There was a splash, mind-numbing coldness, and frigid water gushed over Ace's head, filling her ears and nose. She was plunged into a dark and breathless world.

Terrified, she strained for the surface, which she could still make out as brightness above her head. Weeds curled around her, trying to tie her to the bottom of the river. She swallowed water at first, but then calmness stole over her. The woman would save her. It was simple. She just had to get to the top so that she could be seen. As soon as she relaxed, her natural buoyancy took over and her head quickly broke the surface. Her feet automatically started the thrash up and down in the water, keeping her afloat. The current swirled around her, trying to drag her off with it. The bank wasn't far away and she made for it, but she knew she wouldn't be able to get out of the water unaided. The edge of the bank was two feet above her head. She paddled frantically, trying to stay by the bank as the heavy water tried to pull her away downstream.

A face peered over the edge at her. The woman. She leaned down and tried to reach the dog, but Ace had to struggle a bit more to bring herself within reach. She thrashed madly and inch by inch managed to get close enough. Then she felt her collar grabbed and held, and she twisted to and fro slowly in the current, anchored by her collar. After a few moments the man's arms appeared, also reaching down to her. Ace felt herself lifted a little bit, and as the heavy weight of water cascaded from her fur, she became miraculously lighter, so that between the three of them, they managed to drag her to safety. Two humans and one dog all collapsed onto the grassy bank, and Ace licked the hands of her rescuers gratefully.

This adventure proved to the dog that she and the woman were tangled together forever. This knowledge was so pleasing to her that she was able to finally let go of her bad start in life, and the cruelty that had been shown her. Ace felt that her life was moving further along on the right path every day.

CHAPTER 9

Repaying Debts

I felt that time was proving that we were all there together, for each other, for various reasons. We lived in Norfolk at this time, with its wet lands, broad waters and surging, canal-like, rivers. Norfolk is a fairly flat and low country, without the charm of rolling hills, but this makes for big wide-open skies. Sunrises and sunsets there are hard to beat. There were many lovely walks near to where we lived, and most of them were near a river or waterway of some sort.

One day we took the dogs for a walk along a footpath next to the River Waveney, just outside the town of Beccles. It is a fast-flowing, tidal, deep river, with undercurrents. In fact several people holidaying on boats have actually drowned there after falling in and disappearing under the water. It's quite a dangerous stretch of water. However, our dogs had never shown any signs of wanting to go swimming up until then, and the pathway was clearly defined, so we weren't really concerned about the water, until Ace disappeared into some bushes and to our horror, we suddenly heard a mighty splash. I'll never know what possessed her to jump into that water, or whether perhaps she fell in, but she ended up in there just the same.

My first thought was to panic. I knew that people had been swept way in seconds, caught in the weeds and had died very quickly, only surfacing miles away when the currents finally trapped their bodies against something. I threw myself through the bushes, with Tony hot on my heels. I lunged out flat on the edge of the riverbank and peered fearfully over the side. If we lost sight of her, she might never be found until she washed up dead. The water was a good two feet below the level of the bank, the edges were smooth and sheer with no purchase for paws or hands. To my relief Ace was right there below me, frantically 'doggy paddling' against the pull of the tide. All she could do was hold her position, just her nose and ears above the water, she couldn't get out unaided, and she would soon tire and be whirled away.

I leaned down as far as I could, and Tony grabbed my legs to stop me sliding in. The noise of the rushing water was deafening as its green, roiling mass surged inches past my face. My reaching fingers stretched for Ace's head. She was just out of reach. I desperately leaned further, trusting my husband to hold me.

I called to her, 'C'mon, girl, come on!" Ace made a final effort, lunging towards me, and just as I thought it wasn't going to work, my fingers snagged in her collar. I twisted it round and round so that it couldn't pull off over her head, almost choking her, but it was the only way. I couldn't pull her out though. She was too heavy. All I could do was hang onto her. There we were, stuck like that; me lying on the bank, with the most part of my body dangling over the rushing water, my fingers tangled in a death-grip in Ace's collar, constantly being dragged by the tide, with Tony holding my legs. I was just starting to think I was going to have to go into the water and take my chances with my dog, for no way would I have let her go, when Tony started to clamber over me, using my body as a sort of ladder. His weight holding me in place, he reached over the top of my head and with his long arms he stretched out and grabbed a handful of dog. I don't know how he did it, but he managed to pull her up, over the top of me, while still stopping me from sliding in. As she came out of the water, the weight on our arms eased and we were able to drag her over the lip of the bank. Finally, we all collapsed on the grass, a soggy, breathless trio. *Well,* I thought, *if she doesn't trust Tony completely already, she will now!*

It's hard to explain the bond that the three of us had between us from that day, but some people will know exactly what I mean.

Most people love their dogs, but much as we loved Nyssa and Peri, what we had with Ace was totally different.

A few months later we all moved to Somerset. We'd loved our time in Norfolk, with its big skies and open scenery, but we'd had enough of the flatlands and fens, and wanted some hills to climb. Peri and Nyssa were getting older too, and we thought a smaller garden, with fewer dangers, would be better for them, so we opted for a rural bungalow with a little garden, backing onto open fields.

There were other reasons for our move too. Tony had been suffering in a job he hated for too long. It was time to do something for his sake. He'd always been the one to struggle with the daily grind, and our priorities had to change. The move meant giving up the land and the sheep and horses, but it was worth it to give Tony a better quality of life. Sky, my lovely Welsh Cob, who was not fit to be ridden by this time, was of course kept, and he lived his life out in retirement, staying at first at a friend's yard in Norfolk, and then a few months later, once we were settled in, he joined us down in Somerset.

I'd had a very odd personal, past life experience happen to me, which had totally convinced me of the reality of past lives (for the full story, see my book *Souls Don't Lie*), while we lived in Norfolk, and I was starting to wonder more about Ace and any possible connection to Snoopy. I'd slowly realized that when we first brought Ace home, she'd seemed to already know a lot of Snoopy's tricks and commands. Also she had the same habit (until she got too big) of lying across my shoulders when I was on the sofa. Her face and the look of disbelief when she realized she could no longer fit there had been comical.

I hadn't been able to make much sense of it before, because if Ace had been Snoopy, I hadn't understood why she didn't trust Tony right away, and why she didn't look the same as Snoopy, if she had been him. But now with my own past life experiences happening, I'd looked deeper into the subject, and had come to understand that when we come back to this earth plane we don't always look the same as we did, and we aren't always the same gender that we were last time. And we don't have all our memories intact. For one thing, it would make normal life impossible if we all remembered all our past lives and all the people we'd known before, not to mention speaking all the different languages from our varied incarnations.

I also learned that sometimes, partners, friends and companions have to leave us, either by dying or by just walking out of our lives, in order to make way for other vital partnerships to form. Maybe Snoopy had needed to leave and then come back again in order to facilitate what was meant to happen next with Ace. Maybe he or I needed to be changed by the experience in order to follow our own master plans.

When people talk of one of their domestic pets being 'almost human', they are probably closer to the truth than they know, because that particular dog, cat or horse, is probably going to *be* human in their next incarnation, and *we* have almost certainly gone through the various stages before we became human. Ace would certainly come into that category. Nyssa and Peri were lovely dogs, and much loved, as pets, but their eyes did not contain the same knowing, the same wisdom, or the same spiritual connection as Ace's did, so the chances are that they would live many lives yet as dogs or other animals.

In any case we were very sad when we lost both Peri and Nyssa to old age over the next couple of years. My horse, Sky, succumbed eighteen months after our move, aged twenty-two. This isn't particularly old for a horse, but he'd had a lot of health problems in his life so it wasn't surprising that he didn't live to be very old. This meant there were just the three of us left – me, Tony and Ace, as our son, Phillip, had flown the nest years before to go to university. So, we started taking more holidays, and of course Ace went with us. She was incredible, and people would even let us take her into quite grand restaurants. One look into those eyes and people were powerless to object. Besides, once inside she would vanish under the table, and not a sound or movement would she make. No-one would even know she was there. We were used to her amazing presence, but other people were always touched in some way by meeting her.

We were on one of our favourite walks one day, through a beautiful wooded, Somerset valley. Bluebells shone and radiated through the trees as they made their way up the valley slopes, and a lovely, rushing, tumbling river roared along the bottom. We often saw a kingfisher darting and flashing through the spray like a tiny aquamarine jewel. The water of this river was shallow, unlike the one Ace had nearly drowned in, so we felt quite safe to let our dog run free.

Suddenly, as Tony and I strolled along, Ace running a little way ahead of us, a female roe deer stepped out onto the track and just stood there for a moment. I was amazed and also a bit annoyed when Ace immediately charged after it. It was most unlike her, that this dog that would ignore all livestock, and lick new-born lambs back to life, took off after the deer like a hunting machine. We just saw a flash as the deer jumped clean over the river and set off into the thick conifer trees on the other side, Ace hot on her heels. Of course Ace came back immediately when I got over my shock and called her off, but it still surprised me how readily she seemed to identify it as viable prey. It was as if she already had that idea in her head before she ever saw her first deer.

Tony knew something else remarkable about Ace a lot sooner than I did, and he kept it from me so as not to scare me. At the time we lived in a relatively modern bungalow, not the sort of place that you'd expect anything spooky to happen in. One evening I was out and Tony was in the house alone with the dogs. He told me much, much, later, after we'd moved house again, that he was sitting doing some reading, when he very clearly saw the shadow of a person cross between him and the standard lamp. Naturally he turned round very quickly to see what or who it was, but there was no-one there of course. Ace, who'd been between him and the lamp was looking right back at him, for all the world, as if she was asking, "Who on Earth was that?"

This sort of thing happened several times at that house, and Tony would often wake up with the smell of a pipe or cigarette wafting through our non-smoking bedroom, or see Ace staring fixedly at nothing. No-one had ever died in the house, but of course we didn't know what the land had been used for previously, and this spirit, if that's what it was, could have been someone who used to walk across the land long before the house was built. Tony didn't tell me while we lived there because he thought it might freak me out, and it might have been right!

It was very interesting though that Ace turned out to be one of those dogs who can 'see' spirits. She would often, quite unnervingly, wherever we were living, stare fixedly at something we couldn't see. Her eyes would follow this invisible presence around the room, and then she'd look at us in amazement. This was presumably another attribute of the advanced soul that she was.

CHAPTER 10

A Close Call

When Ace was twelve years old, we had a terrible fright and a terrible experience – for all of us. She developed a large mammary lump. I remember my feeling of total panic as I felt it, and knew it was a tumor. *Not Ace,* I thought, *please, nothing can happen to her.* We took her to the vet, hoping against hope that he would disagree and diagnose something less potentially deadly, but he didn't. Not only did he agree that it was a tumor, but he also felt that because of the consistency of it, and how hard and solid it was, it was likely to be malignant, possibly fatal. We were devastated, but for Ace's sake we tried to put on a brave face – after all, *she* wouldn't be worried unless *we* were.

We booked a day for surgery seven days later. Tony did some spiritual healing on her every day for the next week. Ace seemed to love it, relaxing totally under his gentle hands. I was doing my own thing, trying during meditation to change the tumor and make it benign. Finally the dreaded day came. It was traumatic to say the least. I've never been able to understand why vets can't have a different method of taking dogs in. Having to drop them off hours and hours before their surgery is scheduled, seems unnecessary. I can understand that if people have to go to work and therefore need to drop their dogs off early and pick them up late afternoon, it's necessary to do it the way they do, but it must be awful for the dog. They have no idea why they are suddenly shut up in a cage in a strange place, not allowed access to their pack, and kept hungry all day. Unlike human patients they can't be told the reasons why it's happening to them. So, if the owner is willing, why can't they be brought in immediately prior to surgery?

In this instance I managed to get the vets to grudgingly agree that I could sit with Ace in the waiting room until the pre-op sedative. I thought that would make it at least as acceptable as it was ever going to be.

The vet asked if we wanted the tumor sent off for analysis after it was removed. He said that if it was malignant, there would be little they could do about it, so we said, no, just take it out. Ace was given her jab, and when she was fairly sleepy, they came to take her. I wanted to go through to the theatre area with her, to keep her calm, knowing how she would hate to be taken from me. I felt that if I left her once she was in the operating theatre, she wouldn't be so distressed, because obviously she was used to being left at home. What she wasn't used to was being forcibly removed from her position next to me, which is what happened. She refused to walk, and so was ignominiously pushed and dragged across the room and out the door, on her belly. After what had happened to Snoopy, all I could think of was, *What if that's the last time I see her? Like that? Being dragged away?* The reason they gave for not allowing me to go with her was that she would have to be 'tubed', and I would find that distressing to see. How distressing did they think I found her being dragged away? As it turned out their excuse turned out to be a lie anyway.

Walking out of the vet's without her was very hard, but I went on to work, knowing that was best to keep my mind occupied, and I knew that Ace would presume that I was still where she'd left me. At the time I was doing a great job that I loved, presenting a daily chat show on our local television station. The vet had assured me that she would be taken straight to theatre after I left her. So, imagine how I felt when I called three hours later, expecting to hear that she was in recovery, to be told that she still hadn't had the operation. They claimed that there had been several emergencies, but frankly, I believe that she wasn't scheduled for surgery until the afternoon, and they had just wanted to get rid of me. I was really upset to think that not only had poor Ace been shut in a cage all morning, wondering where the hell I was, but that the surgery, which I was dreading, still hadn't taken place.

Anyway, there was absolutely nothing I could do (except decide to change vets sometime soon) so I just had to wait and phone again in another three hours. Ace came through the surgery fine, and the best news of all was that the vet said the tumor had quite unexpectedly been straw like, and full of holes, so might not be malignant after all. It was very strange because it had been so solid and unyielding before. We still opted not to have it tested, and just assumed that our healing methods had helped. We would just take each day as it came with our lovely dog.

Sadly, after an initial good period of healing, we came home one day to find that the stitches had burst. The wound became infected and the vet couldn't stitch it again, so they just kept re-dressing it and giving her antibiotics. It was a horrific wound to look at. The skin died back exposing more and more infection, until she had a big hole in her tummy. I didn't want to leave her so I had to take her to work with me, and my viewers were treated to a doggy co-host, sitting next to me on the sofa, wearing a rather fetching T-shirt, tied in a knot under her tummy. This was to stop her licking the wound and prevent it from being caught or rubbed. By then we'd given up on the vet's help and had started treating the wound with the plant, aloe vera. It didn't help for a day or two, and then we realized that with a dog this intelligent and this empathic, we'd been making a huge mistake that was preventing healing.

Naturally, each time we uncovered the wound we were horrified at the sight of it, and the awful, if natural thing, was that we showed it. Ace had become used to being asked to lie on the floor quietly, so that we could see to it. We suddenly realized that our facial expressions and body-language when we saw the wound were frightening her, and this fear she felt was slowing down the healing. We realized from her expression that as we uncovered the wound, she was watching our faces, waiting to see how she was doing, just as a person would.

Correcting our blunder, we went about it completely differently from then on. Every time we uncovered the wound, we told her emphatically, "What a lovely tummy! It's so beautiful!" Within a couple of days the aloe vera started its healing work and the wound slowly closed in, a smaller and smaller hole was left, until finally it was gone. Of course the vet claimed it had nothing to do with aloe vera or healing.

Ace made a full recovery from her ailment, and all that remained to be seen was the fact the she no longer had a nipple for the missing gland, and her skin was smooth where it used to be. She developed a taste for being on TV though, and often accompanied me after that. She was very popular with viewers, and I wondered why I'd never thought of it before.

It became harder and harder to ever visualize the day when we wouldn't have her in our lives. Her narrow squeak with mortality did bring it home for a while, but then we just brushed all those thoughts aside. The next three years were wonderful. Her eyesight and hearing got a bit shaky, but she was still the smiley, happy dog we knew and loved, full to the brim with the joy of life.

However, sadly, of course all good things *do* come to an end, but we still had some time together and another important event to get through.

CHAPTER 11

Distant Memories

As a writer and sometime TV host I had occasionally been approached by less than honest people wanting to jump on my bandwagon. Of course I wasn't a big name or anything, but any amount of success, however modest, seems to breed this kind of thing. I was approached during this time by a man who claimed to be a successful literary and film agent. He boasted a long list of credits, and very impressive big name acquaintances fell easily off his tongue. We checked out a lot of what he said and it all sounded genuine in as much as the people he mentioned were real, and what he said about them seemed to be true.

We were anyway the sort of people who don't habitually lie, and therefore don't expect others to lie with virtually every breath they take, which it turned out he was doing. The names existed all right, but it turned out much later that they were nothing to do with him! It's very hard to get your head around someone like this, they live to confuse and fool you. It's their reason for being. This man (who will remain nameless as he is currently in the hands of the law, and is likely to be for some time) told me that he'd read my story (then called *Ripples* – now re-written and re-published as *Souls Don't Lie* – O Books) and wanted to help me get it made into a film. He said it was a story that should be shared with the world. He appeared sincere, and I had never had any experience of a conman. I was delighted, as you can imagine, and as he seemed real, I signed up with him.

As time went by things got very exciting and it seemed that as well as getting my story out to the masses, I was set to become very wealthy. It wasn't long before I was told by him that a contract was imminent, as was an enormous fat banker's check.

How wonderful! In my mind I was already paying off our son's mortgage and buying Tony a real Spitfire airplane, something he would have loved to own! This scenario happened a few times though, and each time one amazing opportunity seemed to peter out, another apparently even better, rose to take its place. After the third time it happened, though, I became a bit suspicious, but still I kept thinking, *what if?* We had been told each time that it was vital not to 'rock the boat' and try to contact anyone involved direct as apparently the film industry was very paranoid.

But eventually, what saved me from the fate of some other less lucky writers was the nature of my story. His usual trick, as we later discovered, was to make you absolutely certain that your script or book was special enough to make the grade. Then after several false promises he'd suggest that what was really needed was a professional re-write of the script. Of course this would assure success, but it would also cost a lot of money, which you were expected to stump up. The idea was you'd think it was a good investment for hadn't all these big names said your story was a winner? Some poor souls fell for this line over and over again, up to the tune of half a million pounds! There would be supposed re-writes, lost documents that had to be replaced, bank fees necessary to release funds, and on and on. But in my case (and a few others who 'sussed' him), my story was too special to me. It was much more than just a meal ticket. It was a true and meaningful event, and I didn't want it changed by another writer out of all recognition. I would rather it never got told, so I pulled out before he got to the point of asking me for money, which would have been inevitable.

The 'agent's' website announced an impressive list of projects, past, present and future, and it was at this point I slowly realized that there were far too many really. Surely even a very successful agent couldn't juggle that many projects all at once? Then I was contacted by another author and he confirmed that this agent was in fact corrupt. I was told that he was using the names of people like me as window-dressing. The apparent credibility of his 'client list' was also being used to convince aspiring writers to pay this agent a yearly fee to get their books into print or film. I decided to try and get evidence and contact the director who was supposedly making my film, to discover of course that he had *never heard of the project*. The director in question was very glad to be informed before further damage could be done using his good name. Further investigation revealed that all the other contacts that were supposed acquaintances of this man were also unaware of him and had never worked with him, or were only too aware of him and had severed all ties. His projects were all lies. It was a terrible discovery. I broke all contacts with the man and gave a statement to Trading Standards. I also contacted editors of magazines that he touted himself in, and they removed his adverts. This was to cause a frightening and unexpected backlash.

Unbeknownst to us this man was actually a psychopath. My calling him out and damaging his money-making con, fuelled a furious response. It turned out that he had been collecting thousands and thousands of pounds; both from writers and people who believed they were investing their own money in sure-fire projects involving their own books and screenplays. Of course as the house of cards came tumbling down, the money dried up, and I was seen by the con artist as the one to blame. He fixated on me. It started with anonymous phone calls in the middle of the night. They were usually at about 2.45am, and when we answered, befuddled from sleep, all we could hear was a sort of demonic voice, mouthing what sounded like curses or spells. Of course the phony agent was our chief suspect, and that was what we told the police when the calls continued. What the man hadn't realized was that withholding your number doesn't stop a police trace, and with BT's cooperation they easily traced the calls to the 'literary agent's' mobile phone. All the police could do at that point was to warn him from harassing me any further, but they made me a bit uneasy by telling me to call 999 immediately if I even saw him in my home town.

The man knew where I lived because he'd been there for meetings on numerous occasions. He'd also met Ace many times and she'd grown quite used to him. He used to bring her treats on every visit, gaining her trust, which was clever. For a while I was pretty scared of what he might do next to exact revenge, and I avoided leaving our home unattended, but you can only live like that for a while. Eventually Tony and I had to go out at the same time. Nothing happened for a while, apart from my getting malicious emails, which I deleted, and so we started to relax.

Then Tony decided that he should go and visit his mother, who lived alone on the other side of the country. We couldn't both go, partly because of my work and partly because Ace was getting too old to take the long trip or be left at home with anyone else. So, I was home alone with my elderly dog. It was about 2pm on the second day that Ace started getting anxious. At first I thought she was feeling ill, but she seemed fine in herself. She just kept looking out of the window and pacing around. Then I thought she was missing Tony and thinking he'd be home any minute. We lived at the time in a quiet close, a cul-de-sac, so anyone lurking around would be easily spotted. The only thing was, our front garden was pretty lush and at one point I thought I saw movement behind one of the bushes. Eventually I went out and looked, but I couldn't see anyone. At about 4pm a car drove up to the gate and stopped there, engine running. I didn't take much notice as there were shops on the corner and men often waited in our road for their wives to emerge from the hairdressers. But Ace stood by the window staring out at the car. She didn't growl and by then her eyesight wasn't so hot, so I thought she probably thought it was someone she knew. I went to the front door when the car didn't move after about ten minutes, and as soon as I opened the door, the car immediately drove off. I wasn't at all worried. It was broad daylight, and it was most likely just a shopper in the car. Maybe they'd got a bit embarrassed at parking there for so long, or maybe the person they'd been waiting for had come back while I was walking down the hallway.

Just before closing time I nipped out to get a newspaper. It was getting dark by then. I remember the street lamps popping into life as I walked past them. I'd locked the house doors, even though I was only going to be a few minutes. Not so much in case of burglars, but in case someone opened the door and accidentally let Ace out. When I came back something odd had happened. Ace was hiding. She hadn't slept under the kitchen table for months, but after some minutes of anxious searching, that's where I found her. She wouldn't come out. No fuss, she just quietly lay there making it plain that that was where she wanted to be. She didn't have a temperature and seemed bright eyed, so I didn't think anything was wrong. Elderly dogs, just like some elderly people get some odd ideas sometimes. An hour later, she was still under there, not asleep, just hiding, or so it appeared. She had her eyes wide open. Anyone walking into the kitchen would never have known she was there. It was almost as if she was setting an ambush. I went back to the living room, put the lights on and pulled all the curtains, feeling snug and safe. At about half-past eight, I must have fallen asleep, because I had the most incredible nightmare, or so it seemed to be at first.

I found myself walking through a forest with a black dog by my side. The weirdest thing was not just the detail I remembered afterwards, and still remember to this day, but that I was a man in the dream. I was wearing strange clothes, a mixture of wool and leather, with metal studs and buckles here and there. I was aware that a few miles further back I'd been mounted on a horse, but it had run into a trap and broken its neck. We'd been at full gallop and the poor horse had hit a vine that had been deliberately tied across the track. We'd crashed to the ground, tumbling over, and slithered along for what seemed like forever. I got up, but my horse didn't. I was very upset and furiously angry. I'd had the horse for ten years and he'd been an equable and dependable steed, not easily replaced, or not at least for a lot of money, which I didn't have. I'd been walking since then, along a forest trail that I normally wouldn't have used at night, alone and on foot. On a fast horse it was a bad enough road to travel, but on foot, it was very dangerous indeed. The trees either side of the track cast threatening shadows and their depths soon merged into inky darkness that could have concealed an army.

I was glad I had Igraine, my dog, with me. She would give any footpads that might be lurking about, something to think about. She was tall and powerful, with vice-like jaws, part wolfhound and part hunting Labrador. I'd had her since she was a scraggy pup, and she was my right hand. It was she who'd comforted me when my wife, Cherish, had been killed suddenly, two years previously while out hunting. My wife had always been a rebel, and one of the very few women I'd met who liked to hunt alongside the men. During the walk, Igraine had growled a few times at things I couldn't see or hear out in the undergrowth, but in the end, when nothing happened, I'd decided she was alarmed by nothing more dangerous than a squirrel.

I was feeling pretty relieved all the same as sparks of light appeared in the far distance, offering a town or village that would provide a degree of shelter and safety. As I walked along I was thinking about the events of the past few weeks. I'd been driven out of my home by a marauding Baron, Robert, and his army of n'er do wells. In the end I'd had to send the workers packing for their own safety, shut up the house as best I could, and flee for my cousin's home, two counties away. I'd barely escaped with my life. All I'd been able to take with me was a family heirloom in the shape of an eagle brooch, encrusted with precious stones, and I wouldn't dare try to exchange that for anything. One sight of it in public and I'd be signing up to have my throat slit in some dark alley. I was confident that in reaching the town I'd have just enough money left in my purse to buy a room and food for me and Igraine, which would comfortably set us up for the final push to my cousin's the next day.

We came to the small village, and I was glad to see that it had an inn. We went inside, and were immediately enveloped in a comforting miasma of chatter, warmth, and the smell of beer. I felt myself relaxing more as we emerged into the pool of light and civilization. I just about had enough to pay for the room and fixings and the pair of us retired to eat and sleep, not wanting to arouse the curiosity of the locals. I had hidden my brooch in a pouch resting next to my skin, and the feel of it there was some comfort. The Baron who'd routed us was an old adversary. As a Knight I'd been outspoken against his evil treatment of the villains and surfs (peasants) of his Manor. Whilst he was entitled to command their presence and loyalty, he was not entitled to take their wives and daughters and use them vilely – on that we'd disagreed, violently. Eventually my thorn in his side had become too much for him, and he'd attacked us in the dead of night, knowing that at the time my home was virtually unmanned, owing to disease and folk weakened by grieving for the dead – my own mother and father, who had died the day before. We held out for a few days, but the end was inevitable.

There had been a time when I had trusted Robert, and thought of him as my friend. I'd shown great loyalty to him, frequently entertaining him in my home, and for a long time I'd refused to believe the tales told about him by my servants. Igraine had loved him, and he'd always taken care to throw her a lot of meaty scraps from the table. But finally, under weight of evidence brought to me by surfs, I'd had to call him out and threaten to report him to the King. I'm fairly sure he would have been executed, or at least imprisoned. But, before I could act, the plague had struck and most of those who would have sworn evidence against him had died and been burnt. And now I was alone, unarmed save for a staff, and penniless save for my mother's brooch.

I'd been uneasy in the forest, obviously because of the trap that had done for my poor horse, and also because I thought Robert would have sent someone after me, if not come himself. But when nothing happened I decided that the trap must have been laid by some common robbers, and Igraine's presence had made them think better about attacking me. I was sure that if Robert had come after me he would have staged his attack in the depths of the forest where its darkness would have concealed his cowardice. So, I thought myself safe. I was surprised then when Igraine started behaving strangely. She got under the bed – no easy feat for a dog her size, and she refused to come out. Her shining eyes winked at me from far back in the darkness in the far reaches of the cavity under the big bed, and no amount of coaxing from me would get her to come out. The behaviour was most unlike her and I got a bit angry when an hour later, she still refused to come out, but in the end I left her there and went to sleep.

What I didn't know at the time was that Robert had actually arrived at the inn well before me. The trap with the vine had just been a ploy to slow me down. I think he was probably also afraid of Igraine's jaws up close, and thought he'd be safer playing it the way he did, letting us relax and drop our guard, thinking we were safe. In hindsight I could see that only I was remiss in that regard, and Igraine was much more aware than me. It was almost as if she could see into the future, for I had no other idea how she knew he was hidden somewhere in the inn. As with most taverns of the time there were a few secret doors and hidden passages, so that evil-doers could escape the hand of the law of the land. These hiding places and escape hatches were used by smugglers and the like, and the owner of the inn would get a percentage of the booty for providing them.

An hour later I was fast asleep, having given up trying to coax Igraine out and into her usual place beside me. Ever since I'd had her there had never been a night when she hadn't warmed my bed with her cozy presence against my legs. Nevertheless I was so weary that I was soon so deep down in slumber that I never felt a breath of air as a secret door was opened and a shadowy figure emerged. If I had been awake no doubt I would have seen the man's puzzlement, as in his hand he carried a slice of beef, and yet he could see no dog to bribe with it. The figure must have glided across the room, passing through the moonlight that slanted through the window. He must have felt safe as he approached my prone figure, thinking my guardian had been consigned to the stables. His dagger would have glinted in his upraised hand. The blade would have swished as it cut through the air, aimed at my sleeping heart.

The first thing I knew about the attack was when a terrible sound rent the air as a snarling Igraine erupted from under the bed, taking Robert by complete surprise. I opened my eyes and leapt from the bed as her jaws closed around Robert's knife hand. Such was her size that he stood no chance against her sudden attack. He screamed as her fangs sank into his forearm, and the knife spun from his grasp. I picked up the knife and plunged it into him, until his dead limp body collapsed at my feet. Panting I subsided onto the bed, leaving Igraine still shaking her prey.

Finally accepting that he was not going to move again, Igraine let go of her adversary and ran to my side. I fell on her, ruffling her coat and praising her in gratitude for saving me. Not only had she somehow known that she needed to hide in order to protect me, but she had also recognized this man – who had always been kind and fed her – as an enemy. Not only that, but she had also known that she must refuse the temptation of the meat he offered. I owed my life to her intelligence, courage, and her almost supernatural ability to prepare for the attack. If I had been more aware and less weary, maybe I would have heeded her warning. But, anyway, thanks to her, we could go home again and rebuild our lives and those of our people.

Suddenly I was wide awake, back in the present, but the dream was still so real to me. I could feel the rough, shaggy coat of

Igraine under my fingers, and my hand felt the ghost of the dagger I'd wielded. My fuddled mind recognized the similarities of the dream and reality. Igraine had hidden under the bed as a warning, and Ace had hidden under the table. I'd ignored her earlier warnings that all was not right, and so she had decided to hide....and surprise an attacker? Could it possibly be?

It was all too possible, but in any case, unlike Igraine, Ace was elderly, and wouldn't be a match for a man, possibly armed, not without being badly injured or losing her life. I checked around the house and discovered that I'd left the back door unlocked. I couldn't believe I'd done something so stupid. I took a large carving knife from the kitchen and prowled around the whole house checking every corner. I wasn't surprised that I couldn't find anyone, because Ace didn't follow me, but I wasn't going to ignore that warning any longer, so I called the police. As they'd warned me to phone them if there was any sign of the psychopathic agent, I felt justified in calling them in. Minutes later, sirens sounded in the town, coming closer and closer, until flashing lights appeared outside the window in the cul-de-sac. I could hear the comforting sound of radios chattering as they opened the doors, and several policemen got out. They made a sweep of the area and discovered, alarmingly, a set of footprints outside the back door that shouldn't have been there. They were a very common sort of print from a leather soled shoe, and would be no use as proof that any particular person had made them, but I was pretty sure who it had been. After making sure I was OK and could cope, and phoning Tony for me to ask him to come home a day early, the police finally left, but a patrol car stayed parked outside for the rest of the night.

I'll never really know the truth of those events. A few months later the agent was arrested by the fraud squad and locked up for ten years. But, what did my dream mean? Was it my subconscious using a very elaborate way of warning me that I'd missed some signs? I'd had many experiences already where past lives had been shown to me in dreams, but I wasn't sure if this was one or not. Was I really once a Knight and Igraine my dog? Did those events really happen in a past life? Was Ace once another of my dogs, Igraine, and was her hiding under the table her way of reacting the same way that she had as Igraine? Had Ace been calling on her past life experiences to find a way to try and save me again?

A further possible complication, which isn't out of the question, because our past lives are often a tangled web of various characters interacting with us again, usually in an attempt to put the past right, was this. Was 'Robert' once the crooked agent? Had our lives entwined before, and had we been brought back together by instinct, to the same situation we'd faced in the distant past? This time, was he supposed to see the error of his ways and stop trying to take and use what wasn't his, and failed to do that? Had he left those footprints outside the house? There were so many questions, but I'll never know all the answers for sure. What I *was* sure of was that Ace had saved me...again.

CHAPTER 12

The Inevitable, Ultimate Sacrifice

Time passes with our loved ones all too quickly. The most awful thing about dogs is that their life span doesn't run in concurrence with ours. Having Ace in my life was something I would never have chosen to miss under any circumstances, but eventually the time I'd been dreading was bound to come. All I could pray for was that I would be strong enough to do the right thing.

It was 3rd June 2004. Ace was fifteen years old by then. The happy times for us had become rarer because for weeks she had been becoming increasingly incontinent and she was absolutely mortified by this. By now she was sleeping in our bedroom, because she got so worried when she was alone. One night she had an accident on the bedroom carpet. Nearly blind, she had been unable to let us know she needed to go out, or maybe hadn't even had time to do so. It was about 3am when it woke us up. Of course the pong was horrendous and the liquidity of the mess on the beige carpet was terrible. It was strange though, because just like a mother, able to change her own baby's smelly nappy without flinching, so I'd always been able to clean up the same way for my darling Puppy, without discomfort.

No, the mess I could cope with. The most distressing thing was the devastated expression on Ace's face. She crouched, miserable, to one side, and when I invited her to come downstairs with me, her sight was so bad that she wouldn't come forward as she was afraid she was going to walk in her own mess. She couldn't move until I went to guide her past it. Her face was crumpled in embarrassment and misery, and I started to realize what I was doing was a disservice to her self-esteem. I'd been telling myself that I wasn't going to condemn her to death at any price, but in reality I was hanging onto her because I couldn't bear to be without her, and not for her own good.

I watched her that day, seeing my once, brave shadow, now beside herself with worry, every time she realized that she didn't know exactly where I was, which was most of the time. All her life she had followed me closely, protecting me, but now she couldn't hear me and she could barely see me either, and it was making her miserable.

It wasn't quite so bad outside in bright sunlight, when she must have been able to see silhouettes, but indoors her world had faded to one of dark grey shadows on a dark grey background. All she seemed to have left was her sense of smell. I'd got into the habit of tapping her lightly every time I moved. But that wasn't working either. The poor dog's arthritis was bad, and to make her keep scrambling stiffly to her feet every time I left the room for a moment was quite unkind. Sometimes I'd think she was sound asleep and I'd sneak to the bathroom or the kitchen to save her getting up unnecessarily, but then I'd find her wandering around, distressed, unable to find me. When I touched her she would start, and I'd have to quickly put my hand in front of her nose so that she'd know it was me. She still loved me and I still loved her, but it wasn't really enough anymore. I didn't know what to do. Well, I suppose I did know, but I just didn't want to face it.

In my distress, I turned to my son, of all people, for advice. Tony was too close to me, and knew how badly I was going to miss Ace, if she died, to dare be the one to make any suggestions. Sensible as always, Phillip said, "Mum, I know she still enjoys herself occasionally, but just because she has a laugh now and then, doesn't mean she should be made to live such a miserable life the rest of the time."

He was right. It was time. Hard as it was to face it, I knew it was the truth. I called the vet. No way was I going to take her there. I wanted him to come to her home, where she felt safe and send her to sleep, but even as I spoke the words, my mind screamed, "Traitor!" How could I possibly go through with it? How could I be the one to sentence my best friend to death? But it had to be me. I couldn't make anyone else take that responsibility. I told myself, as I'd told others, that the person who stopped an animal suffering was doing the right thing. To keep an animal alive when it couldn't do any of its natural behaviors was wrong. Ace was a dog first, and she was Ace second. If she couldn't run about, sniff, see things, hear things and be fulfilled, or even just stay close to me where she felt safe, then what kind of life was it?

All the same, my mind asked me, "What are you going to do without her? How will you live with what you've done?"

Those of you with special dogs will understand when I tell you that even now, I am crying so much I can hardly type, as I recall my feelings on that day, and the dark days that followed. I got Tony to pick up some ACP tablets, sedatives, from the vet's, because I didn't want my darling Puppy to feel any fear when the strange man arrived. I wanted her to relax and be dreaming sweet dreams as she slipped away. By the time the vet came, I was trying hard to hold back hysterical grief. Ace was lying on the living room carpet, dozing, when he came. She started as she realized someone new had come in, but I leaned down, putting my hand where she could sniff it, cradling her and talking into her ear while the vet injected her. As the vet had moved towards her my soul had cried out for me to stop him, take it back, say it had all been a mistake and tell him to leave her alone. It would have been so easy – for me, that is. Far, far harder was letting the vet go ahead and do what he'd come to do.

I invited Tony to say some last words to her and (bizarrely, it seemed later) he chose to tell her she was a wonderful dog, and that she would be welcome to come back to us any time she wanted. I leaned down then, and said quite loudly, so that I was sure she would hear me, "It's all right Puppy. It's OK. You're a good, **good** girl."

Those were the last words I wanted her to hear, because she was the epitome of a 'good dog'. Those people who rejected her as a puppy would never know that they'd missed the enjoyment of having the dog of a lifetime. They'd missed years and years of joy, loyalty and companionship. The pain I felt as she breathed her last was too much to bear.

After the vet had gone, looking at her cold body, touching her fur, knowing that the dog that I adored every single inch of was gone, was too, too tough. I loved the bones of that dog and her presence had been such a huge light in my life that I really didn't think I would survive the pain of her loss. When I look back now at photos of her in her dotage, I can see her grizzled grey hair and how much her eyes had dimmed, but I never noticed it when she was alive. I didn't see how old she'd become, at the time, because I was in denial of it. To me she was as beautiful on the day she died as she was the day we met her.

We had Ace's body taken away for cremation two hours later. It seemed like the right thing to do at the time. We had a tiny garden, so burial was out of the question, and I couldn't bear the thought of her body being disposed of with other animals in an incinerator, and at least that way I would have part of her at least to make a memorial to, but on reflection it was a bit too quick. It might seem macabre to say I wished I'd kept her body overnight, but that was what I did wish in hindsight. Maybe having more time to say goodbye would have helped. Anyway, the next day her ashes were returned to us. I couldn't believe that my gorgeous, beautiful dog was reduced to a few scraps and ashes. That transition in the space of a few hours from big cuddly personality, to dust, was impossible to accept, but I had to accept it.

In an attempt to make some gesture that would be meaningful for years to come, we went to the local garden centre and chose a beautiful vibrant rose tree, dotted with tight little tangerine colored buds. I buried the ashes in the garden and planted the rose above them. The tangerine rose was appropriately named,

'Shine On'. It felt so right, because that was what Ace had done every single day of her life, and what she would continue to do forever in my heart.

CHAPTER 13

Messages

The next few weeks were grief-stricken. Dogs are in our homes 24/7 for most of their lives, which can be up to seventeen years or so, so they really are a large part of it, so it's no wonder we miss them so terribly. We see more of them than we do a lot of our families. Some dogs are such a great part of our lives that their demise drops us into despair. I just didn't know how to cope with my loss. She'd been my best friend, an animal soul mate, and I couldn't face life without her. I felt guilty. I felt as though I had killed my darling Puppy, even though I knew that given a real choice I would never have taken that decision. The only comfort I had was the knowledge that unlike poor Snoopy, she'd died quietly at home, in my arms.

A few weeks later, a friend of mine, a psychic medium called Ann Hind, was at the house. I was very fond of Ann. She's one of those people that light up a room with their very presence, and she always had wonderful words of wisdom to impart. Many times in my life she'd said exactly the right thing at exactly the right time. Of course I was terribly upset still, and trying to console me, Ann said, "You know, she didn't want to be a dog forever."

She was right, Ace was destined for greater things, for new incarnations as a person. I knew that, but it didn't help my pain. She might live on, but not with me, and I might never know her again.

We went and stood outside, by Ace's rose, *Shine On*. Ann was going to try and see if she could connect with Ace for me. Maybe if I had a message from her, some kind of proof that she still existed, I'd feel better.

What happened was extraordinary. Heat started to build up, seemingly coming from the flowers of the orange rose. It was as if we were standing in front of a fire. It was a silly notion, of course, because if the flowers had got that hot they would have wilted immediately, but there they were glowing with orange, and hot. We could feel the heat turning our cheeks rosy. After we'd become used to feeling the heat, and accepting it as a sign that a spirit was near, Ann got in touch with Ace and told me that she was all right, just missing us. Then Ann said something that made my eyes fill with tears, because she had never known any of the details of Ace's illness and the events that led to her demise. She said, "Ace wants me to say…" she hesitated, saying, "I'm not sure whether to say this, it's not very uplifting."

"Please," I begged her. "What is it?"

"…she says, she's sorry about all the toilets, she's sorry about all the mess and wants to thank you for putting up with it, and taking care of her."

Ann couldn't have known, no-one knew, about the messes we'd had over those last few months. Only Ace knew, and it was typical of her to come through to apologize. God bless her.

Anyway, it seemed it was over. A period of my life that I hoped I'd appreciated fully, was past, never to be repeated. That is the one thing that all losses have in common. We always wonder if we made the most of that person or animal, while we had them. I couldn't have loved Ace any more than I had and I could take comfort from knowing that she'd known it. No more though. I couldn't take it all any more. Although I'd come to wonder if Ace was Snoopy returned to me, I'd never had any real proof, and anyway, I never wanted to go through all that again. I know that the good times lasted far longer than the bad had, but I felt so grief-stricken, for so long, that I wondered if I'd ever get over it.

Unlike with other dogs and the horses, I resisted the pull to 'fill the hole' that Ace's departure had left. I knew I would never find another like her as long as I lived. I knew that if I did get another dog and it turned out not to be so intelligent, so knowing, so empathic, so *sentient*, I'd be disappointed with it, and that wouldn't have been fair to the dog. The same thing happened when Sky left me, aged 22. I'd had him for 19 years. I didn't even try to replace him. I knew it wasn't going to work. He was a 'one off' horse, as Ace had been a 'one off' dog. Having Sky and Ace had been worth it, though. All the pain of their passing was fair payment for the years of pleasure they both gave me. My life wouldn't have been anywhere near as rich without them.

CHAPTER 14

Heads Up

We had no pets by then at all, so no responsibilities, so we decided to take a trip to Arizona in the United States – high desert country. We'd wanted to go to Sedona, a spiritual centre in Arizona for some time, but there had always been too many ties to let us. Now we were free and could go. It was small consolation though.

All I really knew about the town of Sedona before I went there was that it has been voted America's most beautiful town, and that it's *the* New Age centre of the USA.

The town of Sedona itself is in an oasis of green in the middle of the hot, dusty Arizona countryside. Amazingly, Arizona has more mountains than the whole of Switzerland. Most of them are grey stone and the town of Sedona sits in a bowl of these mountains, but it's surrounded by the most beautiful, wind-sculpted red rocks, all of which have names inspired by their shapes. Cathedral Rock, Bell Rock, Castle Rock and Kachina Woman, are just some of them. There are also four powerful energy vortexes in the area, each one near a different red rock.

As we left the Interstate from Phoenix and drove into Oak Creek Village on the outskirts of Sedona itself, we had no idea where the vortexes were, but I suddenly found myself moved to tears. Tony asked me what was wrong, and thinking that I'd just been touched by the mere beauty of the place, I answered, "It's so beautiful."

We only discovered later that we were passing right between two vortexes at the time and the energy had obviously affected me.

While we were there I decided that as Sedona is such a

spiritual place, the trip wouldn't be complete without my having a clairvoyant reading. So I went to one of the spiritual centers in Sedona, and consulted Claudia Coronado, a German woman. My reading with Claudia was to be surprising to say the least. It took place on 13th September, and you'll understand why that's important in a while... It was uncannily accurate, just to start with, and Claudia accurately described the spiritual work I myself did and still do. Tony also felt her assessment of my character and personality was spot on. At the end she asked me if I had any questions. Thinking I should ask the normal sort of thing I asked her if she had any messages from my dear Mum and Dad, both of whom I'd lost some few years previously.

She looked a little bemused and then said, "No, but I have one from your dog."

Tony and I looked at each other incredulously, as she continued, "This big dog is black with white whiskers, was she a Schnauzer?"

"No," I shook my head, "but she would look like one as she was black but her face had gone gray."

"She wants you to know," Claudia continued, "that she is a spark of your soul. You two are united through all time and space. She says, and this is very important to her, *"Today I am young again."*

This was lovely and touching, and I was delighted that Ace was sending me messages. It made me feel less lonely without her. At the time I assumed that by 'young again' Ace meant that she was a young dog again in the form of a spirit, as we all like to think our loved ones are young and free from pain in the next world. It was comforting to think that all her ailments had gone. I had happy visions of her as she was as a young dog, skipping around endless fields without arthritic pain or a single worry about incontinence. I wished I could see her again. I wanted one more cuddle with my Puppy, but as long as she was OK and in a safe place I couldn't really complain. What I'd thought she meant though wasn't what she was saying at all, but it took a few more weeks before I really understood.

CHAPTER 15

Reborn and Revisiting

We'd been back at home from the USA, for few days, and I was drawn to an advert in the local paper. "Labradinger/Springador puppies, ready soon". I was intrigued as to what a dog of that sort might actually be. Of course I later discovered that the puppies were Labrador, cross Springer Spaniel. But Ace was gone, and painful though it was, I had to learn to accept that my daily companion of fifteen years was lost to me. No other dog could ever take her place, and there was no point in trying. It was great to think she was living a whole other kind of life, but I would always, always, miss her. I threw the advert away.

Two weeks later I found the cutting from the paper. Neither Tony nor I had consciously kept it, but there it was sitting in full view on the coffee table. I still wasn't going to get another dog – no way, but nevertheless I found myself repeatedly looking at the advert. How had it appeared there? Was it some sort of sign? Eventually I gave in and rang the number. I simply can't explain why. I was certain it didn't mean anything, I was just...curious. After a brief chat with the farmer on the phone about what a Labradinger was, I asked, for no apparent reason, "When were they born?"

"September 13th" came the casual reply.

The day the psychic had said Ace was young again!

I thanked the man and sat down and thought. Could it really mean anything? Could Ace have meant she was *born* again?

Well, of course I had to go and see the puppies then. I phoned again and made an appointment. It seemed surreal. I often have these moments when I do something that either I don't want to do, as in the case of having Ace put to sleep, or something I'm scared to do, like sitting down cheerfully in the dentist's chair, to things I don't understand the reasons for, but just know I have to do them. I go into a sort of automatic state, and it's like someone else is going through the motions, with me as a passenger. Someone or something else takes over and I just follow through the motions like a puppet.

Tony and I arrived at the dairy farm where the puppies lived and were greeted at the door by a friendly little black Labrador. We were also greeted by a crazy, black and white, Springer Spaniel, from the house next door. It launched itself over the six foot high garden wall, and the farmer's son, who'd opened the door, just about managed to stop the puppies' dad from making a surprise visit. We could certainly see how an accidental liaison might have happened, resulting in a litter of unexpected pups.

The puppies were in a very large cage, strewn with newspapers, in one room of a slightly dilapidated, utterly charming farmhouse. The farmer and his two sons lifted the pups out one at a time and put them down on the tiled floor for our inspection. We were immediately awash with a sea of writhing, gorgeous black puppies. There were seven of them, four female and three male, and all but one of them did the normal puppy things. Wriggling around, jumping on our knees when we crouched down, licking us, wagging their tails like helicopter blades and chewing our fingers. They whined and squeaked, all vying for our attention, and we didn't know which one to pick up first.

One puppy didn't do any of that. She sat, poised and elegant, to one side, quietly aloof and waiting for the melee to clear. When things calmed down, the farmer opened the French doors onto the garden and the swarm of pups shot outside like a black and white tide, for a play, but this one coal black puppy didn't follow them. She finally got up and walked over to me. We regarded each other. She was extremely quiet for a puppy. No jumping, no squeaking, just a calm regard. She clambered onto my knees and settled herself there. She gazed up into my face, making complete and unabashed eye contact. Tony crouched down beside me and she casually flicked a paw onto his arm, as if to say, "Hi, I've been waiting for you," looking directly into his eyes just as easily as she had mine.

The farmer was amazed. "Well, I'm blessed," he exclaimed, "That one, she's called, Lily, usually just barks at people. Usually the bitches in a litter get sold first, and the other three of them have, but she just doesn't seem to like anyone. She usually hides away and won't be touched." Realizing, belatedly, that he might be doing himself out of a sale, he hurriedly continued, "She's just shy I expect. She'll come round when she settles with a family. She likes you anyway!" He babbled on, "I can't give them away; they're good pups, they'll make good working dogs. Both parents are great retrievers. She's yours for £100. How does that sound?"

If the farmer had but known it, the price he was asking for the puppy didn't matter to us by then. He could have said £500 at that point. My mind was elsewhere, on a day fifteen years before, when another quiet and apparently difficult black pup had looked at me the way this one did. Tears filled my eyes. It was silly, surely, but she had been born on 13th September, the day I had the reading with Claudia in Sedona....*No, don't be daft,* I thought, *I don't know what we're doing here. I don't want another dog. Nothing could take Ace's place...*But I looked again into the pup's brown eyes and my heart melted. But, just as with Ace and Snoopy, while I could believe what I liked, there was no material evidence to say this wasn't just a coincidence. I'd never really know for sure, or would I?

Then the puppy wriggled and squirmed, and she turned herself over, presenting me with a chubby, pink belly. She stayed motionless, legs splayed, willing me to see. I did see and I couldn't believe my eyes. She had a nipple missing. It was the same one that Ace had lost during her surgery. This puppy had been born with the same nipple missing, on the very day Ace had told us she was young again! This was no coincidence. The puppy looked at my aghast face, and, well, she pretty much winked at me, as if to say, *Got ya!* Her lips were drawn up at the edges and her pink tongue lolled out. She was laughing!

Ace had returned. I was sure of it now. I shuddered to think that I'd nearly denied her. She was young again, she was a puppy again, just as she'd said. She hadn't meant in spirit, she'd meant, she'd been reborn, literally. She had decided to come back, as a dog, to be with us again. Fate had brought her here and fate had guided us to this place at this time. Fate had not allowed anyone else to take this puppy while I was stubbornly throwing signs into the bin. It never fails to amaze me the way maps are laid out for us and yet how long it takes us to see the way. Still, we did, eventually. I think the farmer probably thought we were bonkers by then, we were grinning so much, but he happily took our cash, and we took our puppy, just as happily.

When we got out to the car, the puppy snuggled down on my lap and nodded off to sleep. Tony and I looked at each other, and laughed.

"Did you see it?" I asked.

"I did," he replied. "That psychic was right."

"She's called, Lily," I said with a smile, "Not that far removed from Chloe, two syllables and ending with an 'ee'. It's not her real name though."

"No," said Tony, "It isn't."

We decided to call her KC, short for Kachina. It seemed appropriate because in Sedona we'd searched long and hard for the Kachina Woman rock, and almost missed seeing it at all. Another of Ace's pet names had been 'Acey', so 'Acey' to KC it was.

It's totally amazing how the universe works. When you look back over incidents like this it's easy to see the plan or map unfolding, and it all looks so obvious.

One of my biggest dreads when I had to make that awful decision with Ace was that she might not be able to find me after she'd died. Knowing how distressed she'd been in this world when she couldn't keep track of me, I imagined that she might wander around the spirit world, looking for me, still needing to be next to me but unable to find her way. I'd cried many tears over than thought. Now I knew she had never, ever, lost sight of me. I was also incredibly touched that she'd chosen to come back as a dog again, to be with me, rather than fulfilling what I suspected had been her real destiny – and come back as a human.

We took KC home, and it was a very strange and slightly surreal experience. She sat quietly on my lap all the way home, just as that other black puppy had done fifteen years previously. When I put her down in the garden, she acted as if she'd always lived there, sauntering around her property as bold as brass. Indoors it was even stranger. She walked to the very spot on the living room carpet where Ace had lain, and walked around it in a circle. Then she looked at us as if to say *No more tears. You did the best thing.*

It was like bringing home someone who'd been in a coma for months, and has slight amnesia. It's the same person, but slightly different. It was a very weird experience watching her face, particularly her eyes as sometimes she knew things immediately, while at others she would screw up her face with concentration, trying to remember. At other times her eyes would pop open in amazement as she suddenly understood something, as a memory leapt back into place. Sometimes these were nice things, but occasionally, as with human subjects, she would have an innate phobia, which wouldn't make any sense unless you knew she had been Ace.

For instance, her life as Ace must have also been what gave KC a phobia of matches and flames of all kinds. Nothing had ever happened to KC with regard to naked flames, and yet she would bark aggressively at a lit match or a candle flame right from day one. The other phobia she had was of the vacuum cleaner. She would run and hide under the table when it came out, even though nothing had ever been done to make her afraid. She also had a fear of traffic – in any form, even bicycles. These kinds of phobias, just as with people, are often brought through from past life experiences.

She seemed to know where all the doors to the garden were (we had three), and liked the same toys that Ace had, which I'd kept out of sentiment. Although we knew she was Ace, she was of course a puppy, and puppies need security in their new pack and surroundings, before you can expect them to be left alone. It's tough to wrench them away from their family and shut them up alone in a strange room and expect them to be happy and quiet, even when they are a dog that already knew you.

We had to remember that all her memories wouldn't be intact and that she still needed our help to grow into a happy, well-balanced adult dog. This is a very important thing that even animal lovers can miss. It's our duty to nurture animals that come into our care. We've been entrusted with special little souls that are relying on us to help them progress. This is why it's unforgivable to make an animal afraid of us. To do that is to block their soul's journey and possibly make them have to come back more times than would normally have been necessary. In the case of Ace, who'd chosen to come back to us again, it was doubly important. She'd had such a tough life before that we had a duty to make sure that this one was as trauma free as possible.

In years gone by, we used to make our new dogs sleep alone straight away, to stop them from being 'spoiled', and that's what most people still do, but I wanted KC to be close to us for a start, as I was sure that if we did that we wouldn't have any trouble. So the bed was put on the floor next to my side of the bed, where Ace had slept in her last months. I lay in bed that night, looking down on my little black bundle as she looked back at me. For the first time in months I felt at peace. When we turned out the light, I reached my hand down into the darkness, and instead of the horrible emptiness I'd been finding there of late, I felt a soft, curly coat, and a warm tongue.

For the first time in months I didn't feel the tears pricking at my eyes because of that empty place next to the bed, and I didn't close my eyes wondering where Ace was and if she was OK. I knew she was OK. I smiled to myself, and wondered what would happen in the night. Would the puppy feel safe and settle as my instinct told me she would, or were we in for a sleepless night as we might normally, justifiably, expect? I heard KC yawn widely, and then felt her snuggle down under my hand, sighing deeply, as if to answer my question.

We didn't get a peep out of her until dawn, when of course she wanted up and out. After a few days, she was so used to her bed, and it was so familiar to her, that the transition to her sleeping in it downstairs under the kitchen table was made without a whimper. Of course in her case, she'd been in our house before as Ace, so that must have helped her too. This puppy had no reservations about Tony, or Phillip, when he came to visit; she was just as sweet with them as she was with me, right from the start.

The first time we decided to trust leaving her at home on her own, I told her, "We're going to the shops." She looked from one to the other of us and then went and sat down in her bed under the table. We were amazed. This was a trick Ace had learned and it was one of the ways she proved her ability to reason. I took it one step further and asked her, as I used to ask Ace, "Does KC want to go toilets before we go shops?" She seemed to consider for a moment, then yawned and lay down. And that was that. Right from day one she would tell us, just like Ace did, if she needed to go outside and relieve herself or not before we left her shut in the house. She never made a mistake.

We soon discovered that our newly reborn dog had another talent. She could read energy. When a new person came to meet her, she would behave in a most un-puppy-like way, standing back and refusing to interact until she'd had a good look at them.

Then it seemed she could read their energy, because she could select the people that she used to know, and greet them like old friends, whereas she was very suspicious of people Ace had never known. I don't think it's really possible that she actually recognized people by sight that she had known as Ace, because she would surely have fragmented memories. It wasn't scent either, which a dog would usually use to recognize people, because she always stood a couple of yards away from them while the 'examination' was going on, and made no attempt to sniff them. I think she computed their energy, and read that pattern as something she had encountered before, or not.

I used to think that when we died, we were in spirit, lost to the world, unable to communicate or interact with it ever again, and that was it. Then I'd come to realize through personal past life experiences that not only do people come back, but dogs can too, and of course cats and horses and other animals. However, I was about to learn a completely new spiritual lesson. I'd thought that you were either in spirit or alive on the earth plane, and that was that. And so as far as I was concerned, rather sadly, now that it seemed Ace was back in the physical as KC, she couldn't also exist in 'spirit' at the same time, and so I'd rather lost touch with her essence, in a way. Because each time we 'evolve' into another body, we are slightly changed, otherwise there wouldn't be much point to it, so KC wouldn't really be exactly the same dog that I'd lost. But then I remembered that Claudia had told me that Ace was a 'spark of my soul', so surely there would always be a connection, somehow.

I asked people, I read books, and discovered that in fact we always retain a part of ourselves in spirit. In other words, while a part of us, if necessary, comes back here to live through new experiences in a different envelope, our vital spark remains in the spirit world, learning from watching the progress of our minds and bodies. This meant, happily, that I could still communicate with Ace's core-self – her spirit, even though the earthly part of her soul was now encased in a new body. This was very joyful to me, because I hadn't wanted to lose touch with her personality, while still helping her soul to experience life in the new body. Soon something happened that confirmed all these things, and the progression was such that everything was neatly tied together.

Ace had always been afraid of thunder (and fireworks) and thank goodness when she came through in KC, she wasn't any longer. It was nice to know that she didn't have to live with that fear. One night there was a terrible storm. I was woken up by the thunder and lightning and I thought, *KC is fine with storms, but this is a big one. I hope she's all right.* The next thing I knew was that KC jumped on the bed, sniffed my face, turned a couple of circles, and lay down in the well between Tony and me. I was dozy, only half awake, and thought it was very weird that she'd managed to open two doors to get into the bedroom. But she was obviously fine, so I drifted off again.

Of course, in the morning, KC wasn't in the bedroom at all; she was still in her bed in the kitchen, with two closed doors between us. It had been Ace's spirit coming to tell me that she wasn't afraid

any more. That sort of thing happened again – once at the same house, and once shortly after we moved to a new, lovely place with an acre garden. Being me, I'd worried – would Ace's spirit be able to find us now that we had moved? Then one night a dog jumped onto the bed. This time it sniffed Tony's face then lay down. He recalls distinctly feeling the bed covers get pulled down over his legs as the weight of the dog settled, but a few moments later he reached out his hand and there was nothing there.

This time I'm sure, her visit was to let us know that our moving house was no problem, she could still find us if she wanted to.

If you've never had any of these kinds of experiences, and don't believe that a part of every soul stays in spirit, this may make you wonder if KC is Ace after all. You might think all the signs I'd had were just coincidences and wishful thinking. If I'd needed any confirmation that all I believed was true, I got my wish. A few weeks later a lady called June-Elleni Laine contacted me.

She was a psychic artist. We'd never met at that point, and she had no idea that I'd ever had a dog at all, let alone what kind of dog it was. She totally blew me away in the first instance by telling me she'd been asked to contact me by a black Labrador cross German Shepherd that was in spirit. This cross breed is not one that readily comes to mind. The chances of her guessing Ace's parentage so accurately are virtually non-existent. But that wasn't all there was to it. She also said she'd attached (to her email) a picture the dog had inspired her to draw for me. I opened the attachment with shaking hands, knowing that this drawing could change my life. The black and white sketch was, very clearly, a drawing of KC. It was an exact replica of a photograph I had of KC when we first got her. Ace couldn't have said any clearer, "Look, this is what I look like now!"

Today, one of KC's favorite moments is when she and I have a soppy cuddle. She loves the closeness, and at these times it's when I feel Ace's presence most clearly. The best bit for her, and the moment that makes her close her eyes in bliss, is when I whisper loudly in her ear, "It's all right Puppy. It's OK. You're a good, **good** girl." Those words mean a lot to both of us. KC and I are inseparable now, just as we were when she was Ace.

That bond can never be broken, not by life and certainly not by death, and that brings comfort. She lies at my feet as a write, and we will go forward together. One day that moment of parting will come again, it's inevitable, but I hope this time I will face it with a sense of adventure, knowing that me and my girl will have many more adventures together. She mirrors me and she keeps me balanced, because however well I might act and by doing so fool other humans into thinking I'm OK when I'm not, it's impossible to lie to my dog. KC senses any tension in me immediately. Energy travels, as my favourite dog rehabilitator, Cesar Millan, says.

CHAPTER 16

Another Life with KC

Of course by this time I didn't need any convincing that past lives existed, or that some people and animals share a soul bond that continues lifetime after lifetime. Not totally convinced that the nightmare I'd had was actually a past life memory, and anyway sure that I would still find another previous life or two that we'd shared, I decided to delve deeper into both our pasts.

By then I was quite an expert 'subject', having been hypnotized many times, and I regressed easily into the distant past. I am also able now to access my 'past life angel' quite readily (for more about this see my book *Past Life Angels – O Books)*. This is the being that guides us through our lives and counsels us in the times in-between lives, and because of my strong connection I can be quite specific about which particular lifetime I go to.

In this case, of course, I wanted to find one that had involved Ace. I'm sure there were many lives involving Ace that my angel could have chosen to send me to, but it was important that I went to one that would tie up loose ends for me.

It turned out that one such life took place on the Great Plains of the America. I was unable to get the year of this lifetime as those sort of things were not important in any way to the Cheyenne boy I was at the time. It obviously must have been after horses came to the land, brought by the Spanish, and before the outrageous removal of the Native Americans to the reservations, so some time in between these two events in the 1800s.

My given name was Makeeta (Little Man), and it's one I hoped to outgrow. I was short for my age, small boned, and that's why I was so called. I was born under the Full Moon, which should have made me special, but it seemed I was anything but. I longed to be someone else for my whole life. All around me men and woman were fulfilling their birthright, while I stayed like a man in a child's body. My mother would tell me that I *was* special and had a destiny to fulfill, but I didn't feel it.

My mother was He'ohma'heo'o (Medicine Woman), a magical and amazing healer. People would come from far away, even from other tribes, for her to heal them of sickness or injury. She would chew roots and spray the juice over their bodies, and purify them in ceremonies. More than once I saw her bring a sick person, who had already gone to meet the Great Spirit, back to the world. Some said this was wrong, and that once souls had taken the great leap, they should be left alone until they chose to come back, but always when their loved ones died, these would be the ones who begged my mother to help them.

She was beautiful with round eyes, a narrow nose and full lips. She was tall and had the wide hips that men prized for bearing their children, and her hands were strong and gentle. She was special. I was just her son.

My father was Hotoavêsehe (Buffalo horn). He was a very brave man and I wanted to be just like him. He had been given his name at the age of fourteen. He'd been on a hunt, when a rogue buffalo bull charged his pony. The pony had fallen to its knees as the buffalo's head crashed into its shoulder and had pitched my father over its head. Before he could get up, the buffalo speared him in the belly with its horn. Men rode to help him, but before they could reach him, rather than die, my father had jumped onto the charging bull's back, grabbing its horns and thrusting his knife deep into its neck. He was awarded many prizes for his heroism, including his own pipe bag. He eventually became a member of the Council of Forty-Four, the highest honor.

Hotoavêsehe was tall, taller than most of his family. He was powerfully built and had an intelligent mind. He had thick hair, a hooked nose, and a flat belly. He was special. I was just his youngest son.

My brothers had all come of age and proved their honor. One of them was the best bow-maker in the tribe and the other the best hunter. They were both tall men, powerful, and respected. But I wasn't big or strong and it was hard to be taken seriously by my family. I had small bones and my hands and feet were smaller than my sister's, which brought me great shame. My hair didn't grow straight, but waved and curled like a twisted branch. My eyes were lighter than the rest of my family, with gold flecks. My nose wasn't straight or hooked, but curvèd. My brothers were special. I was just their brother.

My sister was beautiful. She was already married at thirteen years old and was getting ready to give her husband a son. She had been a chaste girl, and much sought after as a wife. Her belly was swelled with the baby, so much so that it was obvious her child would be no 'little man'. She too had wide hips like my Mother. She walked proud and tall without fear. I was merely her brother.

I laughed when I was affectionately teased by my family, but deep inside I was burning to prove myself. Life was good despite my being too small. As the dawn rose the village did too. The women would light the fire and collect water, while the men and boys bathed. Then we'd go and bring the horses back to camp, to be greeted by smoking pots and delicious food. We'd be told any messages that had come to the crier and then the men would hunt and the children would go and swim or play. Later, as evening fell we'd dance and sing, and the storytellers would enthrall us with their tales and legends. My people call themselves 'Tsistsistas', which means beautiful or real people. The name Šahiyenan (Cheyenne), was given to us by the Sioux. This word means 'people of a different speech'. I loved my people and the Cheyenne life, but I always felt something was missing in me.

I was a bit of a loner, and often afraid, and always trying to stifle my fears. I wasn't brave at all. For instance, I had been told as a small child that I must never lose my 'navel amulet', given to me at birth, for they told me that if I did I'd be forever searching for my soul, and that thought filled me with dread. So much so that I would touch my amulet where it hung on my belt, many times a day, and at night I would spend a lot of time searching before I decided on a safe place to hide it. One of my abiding memories was that every evening I would try in despair to think of a safe place to hide the amulet, and worry always that someone would find it while I was asleep and then be able to steal my soul. My brothers and parents and even my sister, laughed at me for my fears, saying no-one would *dare* steal their souls!

I wore little clothing; a buckskin breechcloth that threaded through my belt, back and front, hanging down both sides. Soft deerskin moccasins were on my feet. I wore leather bands on my arms. In winter I also wore a buckskin shirt and leggings for warmth. My black hair hung wild and free about my face and shoulders. I didn't like fancy braids and binding – it would only make it curlier, I thought. I spent many hours fringing my clothes, and trying to make them special with beads and feathers. I wanted to be different and stand out in the crowd by being seen as special, and not just because I was small.

I waited and I prayed to the Great Spirit for the day to come when I would have my own pony, for then I would be taken seriously. Our people hadn't had horses forever. They were one of the few good gifts the white man brought with him when he came to our lands. We used to live in earth lodges and stay in one place, but with the coming of the horses, and the white man, we had started living in tipis, which could be easily packed up and moved. Buffalo were declining in numbers as the white man hunted and killed them, making way for their huge herds of cattle. So we kept moving, following the buffalo herds that had once been all around. Other displaced tribes also caused us problems as they were driven onto land that was once ours.

I had learned to ride when I was about six years old, but I wasn't allowed my own pony yet. My family would have to admit that I rode well and handled the ponies with confidence, but they didn't consider me man enough to have earned my own. Instead, after I had learned to ride the ponies, they let me choose a puppy. From a whole litter just one dog came to me. I decided to accept her because like me was small for her age, grey and shaggy-coated, much like a wolf, with amber eyes. I called her 'Peyote' after the root my mother used in her healing, because she looked ordinary like the root, but to me she was really magical, like the Peyote plant was magical in my mother's hands.

I made Peyote leather harnesses and collars trimmed with beads, shells dug from the soil and strips of colored leather, and used them to strap my belongings to her. I would lead her around the tipis, and get her to carry the packs to my play camp, pretending she was my horse. I'd get so lost in this game that I'd say the wrong things out loud and make myself a target for laughter. Other young men threatened to rename me *'Boy with dog for horse'*.

Peyote and I grew up together and learned together. After two years, the other boys didn't dare laugh at me, because my little runt of a puppy had grown into a big and fearsome, rangy, wolf-like animal, with the biggest teeth. She would bare them at the boys who made me angry and they'd back off. It made me smile. Her coat grew rich and thick enough to keep out any weather, and she would swim every day, even in lakes and rivers that were frigid. I wished I could grow as much and as fast as she did. Sometimes I would dream that I could shape-shift, and in my dreams I would run like the wind across the plains, on four legs instead of two. Sometimes in my dreams I rode astride a horse that flew.

One day, when I was twelve years old and on the very day of my birth, everything changed forever, but not in any way as I would have wanted. I was so angry with my family that day. The last words I spoke to them were in anger and this was something I regretted. I thought that by twelve years old I should have been going hunting with my father and brothers, but they teased me and said that I was still only the size of an eight year old child and refused to let me go. When they left me behind with the women and children early that morning, I was so embarrassed and angry, that I went off without saying goodbye or telling anyone where I was going, heading into the wilderness. Peyote came with me, carrying my belongings.

Just one voice called after me as I crept away with Peyote. My grandmother saw me and called out, "*Makeeta! Eneoestse!*" (*Little Man, stop!*) but I ignored her and ran. She just wanted me for chores and I wasn't a child or a woman. She didn't realize I wasn't going to come back, not for some days anyway. I thought my family would get worried about me when I didn't come home that night, think me eaten or lost and dying of hunger and thirst, and then they'd be amazed when days later I came home by myself, safe after all. I'd show them that I was old enough to become a man. I'd teach them to respect me. I'd make them see that I was special too.

It wasn't as easy as I thought to stay away from camp. My little 'horse', Peyote, carried my water skin and bedroll, and we walked for hours and hours. We got very hot and soon ran out of water. If we hadn't come across a river, we might well have died of thirst. The river was wide and shallow, tumbling over its rocky bed. Lush trees bowed over its edges as if they were trying to dip their heads into the cool water for a drink, and birds waded in the shallows. Peyote and I drank our fill and then swam and played in the river, and eventually I decided to make camp right there next to the water. After dark, many animals came to the river to drink. Soon I could no longer see them, but only hear the sounds of their night cries. Off in the distance the sounds of coyotes howling made me feel cold.

That night I hardly slept at all. The sky was so vast above me that it made me feel even smaller than ever, and vulnerable. As it got darker, I felt more and more alone and afraid, but I was determined not to give in and run sniveling back to camp like the child they thought me to be. Out on the empty plain I was amazed that it wasn't quiet as I'd imagined it would be at all. The sound of the river was comforting, but I could also still hear animal grunts and squeaks. Occasionally there was a high-pitched scream as if something had met its death in the dark. I lay awake listening to every sound, and every sound seemed to me made by some wild animal sneaking up to eat me. Peyote caught my mood and growled and whined at every sound and shadow, making me even more afraid. Each time I started to drift to sleep, she would sit up and sniff the air, her hackles rising on her back, and I could never see what she could sense.

The sky was so dark it was impossible to tell how far away the stars were and they bore down on me like thousands of wide open eyes. I had to sit up and stare out into the night, my senses straining, and my wide eyes out on stalks as I tried to decipher the language of the shadows. I started to shiver and pray for morning, which was still hours away. Eventually, after a few sleepless hours I gave in and lit a fire. I hadn't wanted to because I thought that the people of my tribe, who would no doubt by now be searching for me, might see it. The last thing I wanted was to be dragged back to the camp like a frightened little child. I wanted to go back when I was ready, on my terms. But, I had to have the comfort of the fire's warmth and the light it gave me. I'd gathered some dry wood, just in case, so minutes later I sat, staring into the flames, but I constantly looked around as the shadows that danced from the fire made me think something was sneaking up on me. I searched the blackness outside the firelight, hoping not to see green or red eyes glittering back at me. I wrapped my arms around Peyote, hugging her to me, her thick fur as comforting as a blanket. Finally, I fell asleep, curled up with my dog. I survived the night, and when dawn trickled over the horizon like melting honey, I woke up, and I felt great. I felt I'd proved myself. I was a man! Feeling braver, I collected berries to eat and drank some of the icy cold water from the shallow, fast-moving river.

Much as I felt nervous during the nights, I also got bored during the hot, dusty days, and often thought about making my way home, but I kept thinking someone would soon find me. I decided not to roam any further and stayed by the river, thinking that would be where they'd look for me. No-one appeared. I whittled some sticks into tiny totem poles, sang songs to myself, and Peyote and I followed animal tracks, pretending we would catch them, kill them, and take them back to camp; heroes, hunters. Two days passed. I ran out of food and got hungry. Eventually, Peyote caught a rabbit, and we skinned it, cooked it and ate it triumphantly together by the fire.

Still no-one came to take me back. I was puzzled. I knew they cared about me and I hadn't covered my tracks that well. It never occurred to me that my family and tribe might be in trouble. They were all so brave, so strong, so capable, and I was so small and childish in comparison, I couldn't imagine them not being able to cope with whatever life threw their way. But I still couldn't understand why nobody tracked me down. For a while on the third day I thought maybe they were playing tricks on me, hiding, watching me. Maybe they were going to try and scare me to teach me a lesson. Whatever was happening, I decided it was time to go back, walking tall, and if they *were* watching me, they'd see that I wasn't afraid. I set off early that day and retraced my steps, coming into sight of the camp around noon. From far away everything looked normal. I could see the rounded tops of the earth tipis and tendrils of smoke from the fires.

I walked along, cocky, thinking I'd shown them I was a man, and waiting for the relieved uproar my appearance would cause. But as I drew nearer I saw the smoke was coming not from the smoke holes at the tops of the tipis, but from the tipis themselves, and I started to run. There was no sound, and no movement apart from the flames. I stopped, and caught my breath, staring, listening and trying to make out what had happened. I ran on into the camp. Most of the tipis had been set on fire, not burning very much because the skins held moisture. But they had shriveled and twisted making themselves into grotesque shapes. The ground showed signs of many unshod horse prints, but there were no people anywhere, not dead or alive.

Eventually I found them, all dead, piled in heaps, burned and desecrated. It must have been a rival tribe or the hetane (white man). The mutilations looked ceremonial, but that could have been a trick to make it look as if another tribe had done it instead of the aliens. There was not one single person alive. I finally found the bodies of my family. My magical, mysterious mother, my brave father and the brothers and sister I'd loved, all rendered not so special by death. Some had been killed with bullets, some by knives. I cried over their bodies and thought my life was over. I peered into the ruins of every tipi, but there was no-one alive. I was alone, the only one left.

I knew it had happened before. We had been recently told the terrible news of a massacre of my people by a white leader and his many horse soldiers. They had attacked the peaceful Cheyenne camp of Black Kettle, White Antelope, and War Bonnet at Sand Creek. It had been full of children, women, and old people who weren't able to defend themselves. They'd killed nearly two hundred Cheyenne and Arapaho people that day. Their mutilated body parts had been taken as trophies by the soldiers, just as had happened at my village. It looked as if we'd fallen prey to the same fate that overcame the people of Sand Creek, and this time they had killed the men too. The horses and dogs had gone, stolen or scattered. It was just me and Peyote.

I spent hours dragging the bodies of my family from the bloody pile, and covered them with a rock cairn. Then I sat down in the dust, leaning against a ruined tipi, and unstoppable tears rolled down my cheeks. Suddenly I didn't care if my family had thought me a child. I would have gladly agreed that I was a child at that moment, if only they had come back to tease me. I didn't care if whoever had done this came back and killed me too. I didn't care if I lived or died. Nothing mattered. Peyote stuck her nose into the palm of my hand and snuffed at me. I stroked her head. My only friend. She mattered.

Then I heard something rustling around in the undergrowth. Peyote growled, her fur standing up on end. We crept towards the sound together, she with teeth bared, while I picked up a broken spear and held it out in front of me. There was no movement. I shouted and jumped up and down. Still nothing emerged from the bush. I cautiously parted the twigs to see what was there. It was a foal, a colt, white, dirty, hungry, about ten months old. It had obviously been left as being too young to be of any use (as I had often felt myself to be) or had been driven off by the raiders and had now come back, seeking its dam. The colt whickered as he recognized possible help in my human scent, and stood trembling and weak as I passed my hands over him, searching for injuries. He was unhurt, like me, and frightened, like me. We were alone, but together. Peyote stopped snarling and licked the colt's nose in a gesture of friendship. At last, I had my own horse, but I'd lost far too much in payment for it.

The colt was pure white under the dirt, with a dusting of black spots on his rump. I was able to find him water and food, even though he would have preferred his dam's milk. For a few days I wondered if he'd live, but he was tough and he survived. For a while I just stayed around the camp with my dog and horse, thinking that perhaps some of the tribe might have survived and might come back to look for me. Then as they didn't come, I started to be afraid that the killers might come back instead, and now with my companions, life had some meaning again. It was a dismal place that I had once called home. The dead bodies started to rot, and the three of us had to hide when wolves came to feed on them. Then carrion birds came to feast. I knew I couldn't stay. For one the raiders might come back, and I didn't have the strength to bury all my people, so I was dishonoring them just by being there seeing their bodies rotting on the ground.

So, early one morning, when I was feeling stronger, and with my colt getting friskier as his health returned, the three of us left the camp, not knowing where to go, but knowing we had to leave. In the end I decided to follow the trail my tribe would have traveled to their next campsite, had they been alive. I made a travois with poles and skins, and packed as much dried buffalo meat, grain and water as I could on it. My foal was just big enough to drag it, with some help from me. It was a strange three-way relationship, because we all relied on each other. What was also strange was that my foal needed no training to play his part in our survival. It was as if he was had already been trained before he'd been born. I never needed to guide his steps, and never needed to tie his head, because where I went he would follow.

For two years we roamed the plains, not calling any place home, and not calling any man friend. I learned to hunt and trap small prey, with Peyote as my teacher. She had changed as soon as we left the camp. Instinct had kicked in and she quickly became my dependable provider. I could have forgiven Peyote if she'd left us and gone off to find a new pack. After all, she was able to feed herself right from the start, whereas I was dependent on her to feed me too. My colt could soon feed himself too with the rich grass, but despite never having so much as a rope on his neck, he never strayed far from my side.

We both grew, and Peyote was happy to be dog, and not a make-shift horse. Part wolf, part dog, with shaggy, straight, grey mottled fur, she ran ahead of us if we walked, alongside us as we trotted, and later when I rode my colt she raced behind, tongue lolling, as we galloped, her tail flying out behind like a banner. Never once did she threaten to leave us and go and find her own kind, even when their cries and howls could be heard across the plains, and echoing through the rocky chasms. When we heard the wolves howling at night, Peyote could have gone to find herself a mate and pups, but she didn't. She stayed to defend us, and when one night the wolves came after my colt, she saved us both.

We'd heard the wolves far off for days and nights. Some nights they sounded close enough to be worrying. They rarely attacked men, but they could have easily brought my colt down. I kept him close to the fire, closer than he would normally have liked, but he seemed to understand the need. While I could hear them, I knew where they were, so I didn't worry too much, just made sure I had enough firewood to last right through each night as darkness fell. Then one night they made no sound, and then I did become afraid. It was a chilly night, so I'd made a fire early, which was a very good thing. Despite that the wolves slowly crept closer to us. Peyote was restless, because she could hear their breathing among the breezes. My colt was restless because he could see the tiny movements the leaves made as the wolves slunk between them. I was restless, despite my poorer senses, just because my two friends were. I shoved some long, dry sticks into the fire, so that their ends would catch light and make stabbing torches. Peyote and I could have run away to safety, knowing that the colt was what the wolves wanted, and if we left him they wouldn't chase us, but there was never a question that we would.

The fire blazed all night, and the colt stayed within its light, a small boy on one side of him, with flaming torches in his hands, and a snarling dog on the other. Soon I could see the wolves' eyes glowing like hot, green embers in the darkness beyond the fire. The lights bobbed around as the wolves looked for a way into our circle. All through the night we stayed on guard, circling as they circled, never resting, but it worked. The wolves weren't brave enough, or hungry enough to challenge us. They knew they might beat us in the end, but they also knew some of their numbers would be badly injured and the pack would be weak because of that. In the early morning, when mist floated at waist height and the night air took on a glow, we heard the plaintive cry of a deer, and we knew the wolves had found easier prey.

When we passed herds of mustangs, my colt could have run with them, but he chose to stay with his friends. Mares sometimes called to him, but he took no notice. By the time he was big enough for me to ride, he accepted me on his back as if it were a natural thing for him, never bucking or trying to get me off. I called him 'Winged Horse', because he gave me the speed of an eagle when he galloped with me sitting astride his back. We headed for the grasslands, so that my colt would have rich grazing. The colt and I thrived and grew as we slowly learned to be adults, and then we moved on again.

One day we came to a river in flood, but we had to cross it quickly, because there was a band of white men driving a herd of long-horned cattle nearby, and we didn't want to tangle with them. Before I could stop her, Peyote, as was her way, plunged straight into the whirling, crazy river. She swam strongly, but half-way across she was swept away, out of control, downstream and heading for rocks. I knew she'd be smashed against them if I didn't get her out, but what was I to do? I ran along the bank, keeping Peyote's bobbing head in sight, and Winged Horse ran with me.

Peyote was struggling to keep her head above water and even from the distance I could see the fear in her face. Our eyes locked across the surging water and I could see her relax a little as she recognized that I wasn't going to abandon her. I didn't know what I was going to do, just that I must do it.

I ran and ran, and Winged Horse kept up, even though the ground was rocky and slippery for his hoofed feet. Finally the river narrowed and Peyote was brought closer to the bank. I looked ahead and my heart almost stopped because I could see that the river divided itself up, raging between high jagged rocks that channeled and funneled the water between them. Peyote would never make it through the gaps without being smashed to pieces, and I could see no way of getting her out. Beyond the gaps the river reunited with all its parts and turned white and ferocious, so even if Peyote survived the channels she wouldn't survive the wild water. Rocks were strewn all across the river bed and the water was boiling in fury around them. If I was going to get my friend out alive, it needed to be before she was taken through.

I spotted one chance. One gap, nearest to the bank was narrow, and maybe if I could stand in the force of the water I could catch her as she came through. It was stupid, I knew that really, and yet I had to hope. I knew I would never be strong enough to withstand the power of the water and we'd both be dashed on the rocks beyond, but there was no choice. I turned to Winged Horse, really just to say goodbye, and tell him to go and make a new life without us, but I was astonished to see that he was lowering himself into the water. "Wait!" I yelled and ran to him, clambering onto his back. Together, we'd go together, and together we might win. As Winged Horse went into the water, the force of it dashed against my legs where they hung either side of him. When I felt the power in the water I knew that I wouldn't have been able to stand in it alone for a second, but Winged Horse was strong enough, and he had four legs.

The two of us stood in the gap, horse and boy, as the swirling water rocked us, and with the bank on one side and a sharp rock on the other. All the while the water hurled our friend towards us at a frightening speed, her head appearing and disappearing under the waves as they broke. Our only piece of luck was that Peyote was being swept right towards the very gap we stood in. Finally, she cannoned into my colt's legs, and was pinned there against him, and I reached down as far as I dared and grabbed a handful of her neck fur. She scrabbled with her paws at Winged Horse's belly, but he didn't flinch. My heart stopped as the water surged and pulled her out of my grasp, but with a snatch of her powerful jaws she grabbed a mouthful of my colt's tail and hung on.

Winged Horse immediately started moving backwards, to the bank, and as Peyote twisted round, hanging onto his tail, like a squirming fish on a hook, I was able to grab hold of her again and as my colt turned to jump out, I desperately dragged Peyote with us. Without the colt I would have drowned, and so would Peyote. As we reached the shallow water at the bank, I slid off my colt, and it was Peyote's turn to grab my belt and haul me out, while Winged Horse bounded up the bank to safety. It was a day we would never forget if we lived a thousand years.

I had been taught by my brothers to fashion bows and arrows, and spears, out of branches, using strings of hide to bend the bows, and I decided it was time to kill my own food. Peyote became an incredible hunter, and with her to flush the prey out, and me to shoot it with my weapons, together we caught more rabbits and birds than we needed. Later we hunted deer to eat. Winged Horse could smell water from miles away, so between the three of us, we never went hungry or thirsty. We occasionally saw white men, but we stayed away, and we also avoided other tribes, not knowing who might be friendly or otherwise.

Wars had raged between tribes as we were pushed from our hunting grounds by invaders, and land that could support a village became scarcer. I was confused as to who might see me as friend or enemy, so I stayed away from them all. In that way the white soldiers had stolen not only my land but my ancestry too. I could never go back. The three of us, horse, dog and boy, were now my only tribe. Winged Horse was strong and beautiful and I was very proud of him. One day I woke in the morning feeling changed. I knew that Little Man had died, and I was someone new, so I changed my own name to Votoneve'hamehe, (Winged Horse's Owner) and Little Man was gone forever. If my family had come back from the spirit world, they would never have recognized me as the boy I had once been.

I very rarely got lonely for people, and I came to love my life.

I was never short of conversation, because my friends and I were able to communicate without talking. I grew to understand what they wanted just by their body-language, and learned how subtle communication can be. I sometimes thought the invention of language might possibly have been a backward step. With it gone, intuition became strong and I was at one with the land. I had my dog and my horse and I didn't need anyone else, but I did need the two of them, and always would.

Many summers and winters passed, and I lost count of the days. The seasons were no mystery, and yet I forgot their names. I knew I had finally grown taller because I reached higher when standing next to Winged Horse, and I could leap more easily onto his now broad back. My hair grew long down my back and I forgot to hack it back until I was sitting on it. I wondered what I looked like now, and I wondered if the boys of my tribe would still have teased me. We reached the mountains and saw snow on the peaks. We stayed in the green lowlands at their feet, knowing that great spirits lived on the mountain tops and might be angry if we climbed to their homes. Life was easier in the valleys. There was water and plenty of grass for Winged Horse, but the land was too steep for cattle, so the white man ceased to bother us.

As the years passed, Peyote got more gray hair in her coat. Her face grew gray. I knew that one day one of my dear friends would grow old and leave. She was already six summers old on the day that the camp was attacked. We had been traveling for about four years and I didn't know how much longer she might be able to run with us before her limbs seized up. I dreaded the day, but I knew what I would have to do. Winged Horse and I could not continue without her. Our three souls were linked and inseparable. She would not walk the spirit world alone. When the day came for Peyote to leave this world and go to the Great Spirit, Winged Horse and I would take the great leap with her.

When that time came, Winged Horse and I would carry our fading friend and climb a sculpted rock together, and then we three would soar from its top liked a true eagle and its riders. Sailing through the sky together, we would easily leap from this world to the next, following our friend as she had always followed us. It would be glorious.

Sometimes we get signs that we really need at a time when we really need them. I had amazing confirmation of that particular past life memory the very evening of the day I wrote it down. It might not sound like a great deal, but messages from our past life angels are sometimes subtle, as if they're checking that we're paying attention. Paying attention to them is what we're here to do. It's the only way to discover the whole of our true selves, and what we came here to do.

To me, the incident that follows was uncanny and unmistakable. Tony and I were watching a television series called 'Return to Lonesome Dove', as we have a liking for these authentic, and yet fairly gentle, quality, western films. The scene switched to a badly injured cowboy, staggering into an Native American camp, desperately looking for help, even though it had been another band of Native Americans that had attacked him and tried to kill him. He had little choice because he'd been wandering, wounded, getting steadily weaker for hours before he came across the village. The tribe watched him with suspicion as he approached.

I suddenly said to Tony, 'Watch. This is a tribe of Cheyenne and so they will call him hentane, which means white man." Tony had barely looked at me and smiled when the very next thing the Cheyenne man (as he indeed turned out to be) said, was 'Hentane! White man!'

Tony and I looked at each other in amazement. This was not a coincidence! This sign was just to tell me that I had the past life memories right. These sorts of clues are all around us, but mostly we just don't notice them, much to the disappointment of our past life angels, but they keep trying. Once you get into the habit of listening to these angels, you get more and more messages from them.

CHAPTER 17

Signs

There are many animal/human partnerships that transcend life and death. Animals, especially dogs we are close to, reflect our energy. If you are sad, happy, weak, or excited, your dog will know it, and if you need to really understand what your problems are, look at your dog. If your dog has issues, they are probably the same issues you have, even if you don't realize it. Given that this philosophy is true, it makes sense to me that these animals travel with us on our soul's journey, in a symbiotic partnership.

So many people like to have a pet. Most find inexplicable comfort in the company of an animal from another species. It goes much further than comfort. Many of us recognize that we have a spiritual connection with them. In our animal companions we can see the stage we're at in our journey, and they can teach us vital lessons.

The life of Little Man resonated a lot with me. It all made such beautiful sense and reminded me that I still have some of the same issues. By remembering and acting on that lifetime I will be able to iron out some of my negative attitudes this time round. I believe that the dog Peyote, was the same soul as KC, and the pony in that life 'Winged Horse', was the same soul as Sky (the name 'Winged Horse' even links to 'Sky Walker', my horse's full name). I believe the pony was Sky because he and I have shared the same sort of life this time around. He came to me at a time of great grief, when I had just lost my first horse, Baloo, in tragic circumstances. Sky was a sensitive horse and needed me as much as I needed him. He was only three and yet had been broken to haul a cart, and treated, while not cruelly, in a not very sensitive way. Consequently he was a bit 'head shy', which meant he would flinch at any sudden hand movement towards his face. I was very careful to encourage trust in him. Eventually, once trust was established, we did everything together, and my choice of one day events, show jumping, dressage, carnival entrants, and long-distance pleasure riding, are a modern day equivalent to Votoneve'hamehe's journeys in that past life.

Back then, Votoneve'hamehe and his horse traveled many miles together through necessity, faced difficulties together and were triumphant together, gradually healing each other along the way. In a way this is what Sky and I did too. People used to smile at us as we went round a cross country jumping course, because I would talk to him all the way round, egging him on with verbal encouragement, and what's more, he would answer back. Friends could plot our course across the country and the jumps, without actually seeing us, by listening for Sky's shrill little whinnies as he responded to my voice. We have also had many adventures, some of them scary, which replicated some of those shared by Votoneve'hamehe and Winged Horse, just as Ace and I shared some similar to his with Peyote. Their escape from the wolves was similar to my escape from the ram. Ace falling into the river, was very similar to when Peyote got swept away. This is how it sometimes works, similar scenarios are sent to help our subconscious remember our past. If you ever find yourself thinking, *I've done/seen/heard* this before, then you probably have done.

I believe Tony might have been Votoneve'hamehe's father in that lifetime, because of course we go round and round with the same people too. He had all the strengths I also admire in Tony. He's a born leader, but without really feeling like one, or behaving aggressively, just because he retains the ability to think and act sensibly in an emergency situation, when people like myself would be rushing round like headless chickens in complete panic mode. One thing happened to him, which to me, mirrored events in Hotoavêsehe's life. Tony was once employed in the oil industry at Purfleet, in Essex. He was on his way home one evening in the car, and stopped at a red traffic light at a crossroads. A cyclist had gone through while the lights were still green and was moving across the road. From Tony's right came a lorry that had obviously jumped the lights just before they turned green, and he hit the cyclist.

The poor man was thrown clean across the carriageway and ended up on the opposite side of the road, lying on the path, his head tipped back over the curb, into the road. People at the scene reacted in different ways. The lorry-driver, obviously in a panic, combined with his fear and guilt over what he'd done, couldn't face it and he continued down the road a few hundred yards before he pulled up. His excuse, later, was that he wanted to find a phone and call for help. Drivers on the cyclist's side of the road drove past the man's body, actually swerving around his head, without stopping. They gawked, but didn't want to get involved. I suppose they thought that if they did that they might be accused of having something to do with the accident, as the culprit had apparently hit and run at this point. Drivers on Tony's side of the road were stuck behind him as he was first in the queue, so he was first to reach the other side of the carriageway once the lights turned green. So, as the poem goes, 'when all around were losing their heads', he kept his. He parked his car in front of the cyclist, to protect him from vehicles, and set the hazard lights flashing, and then went to assess the damage to the man. As he reached the prone body another man appeared at his side, proving that some other people were ready to put themselves on the line to help. Having watched a lot of hospital TV the other man, quite rightly said that they should not move the injured man, and normally he would have been right, but the angle of the man's head meant that he was choking on his own blood, and he had in fact stopped breathing. So Tony said that they needed to gently move him into the recovery position, on his side, while supporting his head and neck. They did this and the man immediately gasped and resumed breathing. Police officers who came to the house later said that by his calm and sensible actions Tony had not only saved the man's life, but had most likely enabled him to make a full recovery. Of course, when Tony got home, covered in blood, it was my turn to panic!

This incident illustrates why I feel such admiration for my husband, and aspire to be like him, in the same way that Little Man aspired to be like his father, so it would make real sense that they were the same people. Certainly Tony has had past life dreams and regressions where he has lived a life as a Native American.

The past life as a Cheyenne boy also explained why I developed a love for cross country riding from an early age, even though not a single other person in my family was interested in horses in any shape or form, let alone this potentially dangerous, yet fulfilling sport. The reason I was drawn to it, more than any other horse activity was because I loved the notion of horse and rider crossing 'wild country' together, negotiating natural obstacles of all kinds. The Hickstead Derby was the first horse competition I remember loving watching, from a very young age. This was because it had some natural obstacles throughout the course – the Hickstead Bank, the road crossing, and the Irish Bank and The Devil's Dyke, to name but a few.

There has always been something very evocative to me about horse and rider succeeding, together, independent of anyone else. This was what gave me the drive to take myself and Sky all over the county in my little horse-box, to shows and events. It was daunting but very fulfilling. I used to wonder what if… I had a puncture…. broke down on a busy road… ran out of petrol… had an accident. But the pull to be out there with my horse, battling against the elements (even if nowadays they were other motorists and modern-day hazards, as well as the jumping risks, as opposed to rival tribes and packs of wolves), always over-rode all my fears. Luckily nothing like those things ever happened.

Nowadays there is very little opportunity to ride unfettered across open countryside in the UK. I have often thought of going to some sort of 'dude' ranch, in USA, just to re-experience the countryside there on horse-back. It would have to be one that wasn't just for pleasure riding, where you actually do some work, like cattle-driving, so that there was a purpose and meaning to it. I wonder what other memories might resurface if I once more rode across the Great Plains on horse-back. One day, I'll do it, and now that Sky has once more passed to spirit and may have reincarnated again somewhere on Earth, you never know who I might end up riding.

Past lives sometimes explain things so neatly that you can't help but realize that everything is set out, that we all have a plan we're following. The life of Little Man also explained to me why I have always felt like the under-achiever in my family in this lifetime. I would be naturally sensitive to such things, having had that life. I can now see the truth, that Little Man was brave, he was a man, and didn't deserve the low self-esteem he had. How many children could have carried on as he had, despite the weight of all that grief and all the problems he faced trying to feed and care for himself and his pack? I can see that I have no need to feel like the underdog in my family. I have never been one to feel good about what I have achieved and my recollections of Little Man have made me see that maybe I have untapped potential and perhaps I should do so a bit more.

It's also no wonder that in this life (and probably in others too), when I was reunited with KC (Peyote), I had a difficulty in being able to cope with my empathy and sensitivity to the way a lot of people treat animals, and even how many people think of animals. This over-developed empathy has made life difficult at times as I find it very hard to detach from any animal's suffering. Passing a lorry-load of sheep off to the abattoir has the capacity to move me to tears for the rest of the day. No wonder that Ace's departure into spirit affected me so deeply, and made me feel it should be the end for me too. The partnership Little Man had with Peyote demonstrated the connections between the two of us very well. Little Man felt unable to go on without her, not just through normal grief, but through a feeling that when the team was severed apart, that was as far as he was supposed to go with his life.

So, if you are lucky enough to have a bond like I have with a dog like KC or a horse like Sky, you may consider that you have most likely shared several lives with that animal. Bear in mind that you have a great responsibility to treat the animal with sensitivity. If you have lost such an animal, you might also be lucky enough that they will choose to come back to you again as another dog, rather than moving on without you. That is a very high honor to be paid.

Sometimes you read wonderful true stories about dogs that saved their owner's lives against all odds, or despite logical common sense and instinct, and you try to make sense of them. They should make us all think. Dogs normally should have such a strong survival instinct that it over-rides everything else, but sometimes it just isn't the case, and these dogs put themselves at risk, without being trained to do so (unlike a fully trained police dog) in order to help their owner/soul mate.

One such dog was Dorado, a guide dog who was lying under the desk of his owner, Omar Eduardo Rivera, on the 71st floor of the north World Trade Tower, on that fateful day 9/11 in 2001 when the terrorist aircraft hit the building 25 floors higher up. When the ensuing panic hit with thousands of people all trying to flee to safety, Mr Rivera, being blind, assumed he was never going to get out. He struggled to keep his feet and the people flooded down the stairs around him. Amid all the people rushing down the stairs, he and his dog, a golden Labrador, had no chance. Assuming he was going to die and not wanting his dog to suffer the same fate, he slipped the lead off his dog's neck and told the dog to go. The courage in doing that and the dedication he felt

CHAPTER 18

Other Animals in My Life and Strange Incidents

My favorites among our pet sheep were Rosie, one of our original ewes, and Sooty. Even when he was full grown, with magnificent curly horns, I could sit down on the grass and he would lie down next to me and put his head in my lap and go to sleep. Of course, we didn't make the same mistake we had made with Teddy, Sooty had been castrated at a few days old. When Rosie reached the end of her comfortable life, aged just six years old, and arthritis set in very badly, the vet said I was the only person he'd ever heard of who wanted their sheep euthanized with an injection, rather than having it shot. But to me it was an obvious choice. Rosie had always been gentle and sweet-natured. I wanted her to go gently into that good night, and so she did.

Sadly, the same thing can't always be done for horses. It's a controversial subject. Some people say they should be put down by injection, and others say that being made 'wobbly' and falling over, is scarier to a horse than a quick bullet. I think if the horse is down, injured, then an injection is feasible, but if they're on their feet...I think maybe quickest is best.

When you have an animal, it's part of your duty to know when they've had enough of this life. In this instance we had to make a decision over our pet Shetland pony, Smokey. He was in his early twenties, not that old for a pony, but he suffered from terrible laminitis. This is an awful and very painful disease, to the pony it feels as if it's walking on four infected toe-nails. The only possible solution is to restrict their diet of lush grass, which keeps the disease in check if you're lucky.

For years we had managed Smokey's condition that way, but he hated being kept apart from the other horses and would fret and try to push the fence down to get back in with them. But there came the day when he showed no interest in them whatsoever, and that spoke volumes. He just lay there, in pain, not wanting to know about life at all. So, I made the dreaded phone call. I have to admit, that as yet (remember I said I wasn't strong like Maggie) I haven't yet stayed with a horse while it's put down. I think that with a horse the most important thing is that their handler stays calm. They pick up fear and anxiety very quickly. As I knew I wouldn't be able to control my emotions, I thought I'd better stay away, so that Smokey didn't sense what was about to happen. The men were very professional, and after helping to get Smokey to the ramp of their horsebox, we went indoors. Keeping a weather eye on the horses out in the field through a window on the other side of the house, we heard the bolt go off, and we noted that the others started galloping round in a frenzy, hearing the sound two or three seconds later, even though they had often heard shotguns going off in the countryside around them and taken no notice. It was as if they knew. It was as if they sensed Smokey leaving. Maybe they saw his spirit released from its pain, and maybe it was free to run with them again. Maybe they were running joyfully with his spirit. I'd like to think that was it.

When we came out of the house later, a very strange thing happened. I was a bit reluctant to go out, knowing there would be blood on the spot where Smokey had stood. The three dogs stayed in the doorway, instead of roaring out, down to the fields. When they did emerge, they ran as a pack, over to the spot where Smokey had last stood, and they ran round and round it, barking madly at something that we couldn't see. It wasn't just the blood. They had seen rabbit's blood before and not reacted like that. Besides they were clearly all looking upwards, barking at a spot in mid-air, rather than at the ground. It's my belief that they could still sense Smokey's energy, and didn't understand why it was there and yet he wasn't. After a while they stopped barking and gradually wandered off, but it was very odd. It reminded me of some other odd incidences involving animals; other times when animals that have died, sometimes tragically, have left something of themselves behind.

My first horse was Baloo. I'd had him years before, when we still lived in Essex, during Snoopy's reign. I'd called him my little black bullet. He was a fairly common breed, with a bit of Fell pony in him, but he meant the world to me. I'd ridden since I was quite small at riding schools, but never fulfilled my childhood dream of having my own pony. It wasn't until Tony and I had married, and Phillip was born, that my darling husband made my dream come true. Although I'd wanted a pony since I could walk and talk, I was 24 and a mother by the time I got him.

Baloo was bought from the travelers. He was all we could afford at the time. He was cheap because he had part of his lower jaw missing, which made it difficult to find a bit to suit his mouth. He was full of worms, showing the classic pot-belly of malnourishment, and he had long, long shaggy, scruffy black hair – hence the obvious name choice – *Baloo* the bear from *Jungle Book*.

I vividly remember the day I took him home. I was so proud. He'd been bred about seven miles from where we lived, and we couldn't afford a horsebox, so a friend and I decided to walk him. It was pretty strange walking him through the town, through all the traffic, in just a head-collar rather than with the greater restraining capability of a bridle. If I'd known then what I know now about horses, I never would have dared to do it that way, but he was as good as gold. I was a bit put out when we finally got to the yard, because to me this pony represented a dream come true – whereas to others at the yard he was an eyesore, common, tatty and unwelcome. They sniggered about him as he tucked into a stack of hay as if he hadn't eaten for weeks. It was the first hint I got that sometimes living our dreams turns out to be less than perfect, usually through someone else who tries to spoil it for us.

But I had the last laugh, because with good food Baloo grew strong, and his height increased to a respectable 14.2hh. We eradicated the worms, the shaggy coat fell away, and he blossomed into a sleek, magnificent black pony that would jump his heart out for me. We had such confidence in each other that I could even jump him in a halter, bareback. We used to enter all the local competitions, and he soon stopped the sniggers as he steadily amassed a pile of winner's rosettes. He taught me a lot. Having only ever ridden riding school horses before, I embarked on a journey of learning how to care for a pony of my own. I loved him. It was one of the happiest times of my life, and one I will always treasure, but it wasn't to last. I owned him for three short years.

One dreadful day that I will never forget, I was riding Baloo along the road, blissfully unaware of the tragedy about to unfold, and we were on our way back to the stables. We'd had a great ride, and I was mentally promising Baloo a nice feed when we got back. A car appeared in the distance, coming a little too fast for comfort and not slowing down when the driver saw us, but I wasn't too worried. It was a wide road and Baloo was great with traffic. I had no idea how fast things could go wrong, and how fast horses can move in the wrong direction. Drivers often don't realize what they're dealing with when they pass a horse on the road. Horses are easily spooked, powerful creatures and have no idea that cars are dangerous. They are much more likely to be afraid of the perceived threat of a suddenly moving small object, such as a a plastic bag, which poses no real threat at all, than the very real threat posed by a car. The silliest thing up until that day that a driver had done to us was to toot his horn just as he passed by. Of course, having no idea what the sudden noise signified, and startled, Baloo had jumped sideways onto the pavement. Thank goodness there were no pedestrians there at the time. I came across the driver parked up further along and asked why he'd done it. He said to let the horse know he was coming past. Enough said.

The tragedy happened in the blink of an eye. A bird, a leaf, or a bit of paper, I never did know which, crackled amongst the twigs of the hedge next to us, and something darted at my pony's head. It wasn't his fault. Horses are prey animals, with little fighting ability against the lions that stalked them in their race memory, and their only real defense is in rapid flight. Completely unaware of the danger posed by the car, Baloo jumped sideways away from the perceived threat in the hedge. His leap took him into the middle of the road, and his weight and momentum carried him further up the road, before I could do a thing to stop him.

The car was coming just as fast, straight at us. I screamed, 'Stop! Stop!' as I wrestled with my pony, desperately trying to push him back to safety. But it was too late. By the time the car driver braked, the speed kept it plowing straight into Baloo's legs. He squealed in pain as he realized where the real danger lay, only too late. As he crumpled, I was thrown onto the car bonnet, and then I rolled back down into the road as Baloo got up and fled. I had a moment of hope, as I could hear him cantering along the tarmac. Surely, if he was cantering he must be alright. But I looked round, and I could see the unnatural angle of one hind leg as he held it out to one side. I knew at that second that my pony was as good as dead.

There was potential further tragedy looming as Baloo was racing in a panic straight towards the village and more traffic and people. I called out his name, over and over, and he threw up his head and whinnied back at me pitifully. He staggered to a stop and turned back to where I waited. Cantering again in that lopsided way he came back, right into my arms. He thought he was safe with me. I knew better. I led him into a garden to get him away from the cars. The owner of the car pursued me, wanting to know who was going to pay for the damage to his car. He obviously didn't know that despite my pony having gone into the road, he'd had a charge of care when approaching livestock that he hadn't followed, so it was his negligence. In any case I was swallowed at the time by grief, knowing that I was about to lose a dear friend. I asked the driver to call the police, saying I would talk to them. I couldn't bear the sight of the car driver at that moment.

Tony was at work in London that day, and so he wouldn't be able to get back in time to help me, but my father answered my frantic phone call, and God bless his courage, he came to do what I could not bear to do. He came to hold Baloo's head while he was put down. He was a friend my pony knew, a familiar presence to help keep him calm. I would never have been strong enough to do that. My father told me to say goodbye to my pony. I did so, stroking his nose, making sure I would always remember that last touch, choking back tears, and was led away, sobbing, into the house that belonged to the garden. The lady was very kind. It took me weeks to get over the dreadful shock. It would be years later before I understood why sometimes tragedies have to happen and why sometimes friends have to leave us.

I should never have gone so soon to look at other horses to fill the hole that Baloo had left in my life, I but I was taking tranquilizers prescribed by our GP, to help me through the grief, and I suppose I went off in a daze, thinking it was the right thing to do. Almost immediately I found a lovely mare called Cindy. It was obviously a mistake to try and choose a horse while on tranquillizers. Then something very odd happened.

I had moved Baloo to a much nicer yard, with much nicer people by then, and one day when I was there, one of the other horse-owners at the yard, Angela, walked into the stables and said to me, "Who's got a new horse?"

I knew she didn't mean me as by then I'd had Cindy for a couple of weeks. "What do you mean? There aren't any new horses." I answered.

"But it's out in the field. There's a black horse, galloping back and forth down by the trees. It's going potty! It's odd, though, because none of the others are running around with it." She was puzzled, because the same thing always happened when a new horse was introduced. There was always a few hours of excitement, as we'd all gather if we could, to watch the show, while the new horse blended in with the herd. I told her again that no-one at the yard had a new horse, and we both ran outside and looked across the field, but by then there was nothing to see. There was no new horse running around, and the others were all grazing peacefully and undisturbed. We didn't know what to think, but my heart wanted to believe it was the spirit of Baloo, because the oddest thing of all was that anyway, there were no other black horses at the yard.

The next day I got Cindy ready for our first outing to a show, but I quickly realized that it was going to be impossible. She must have had an accident in a trailer at some time in her past, because nothing would induce her to walk inside it. We had had a little difficulty getting her into the bigger horse-box to bring her home after I bought her, but this was much worse. She became hysterical at the thought of going inside the smaller trailer. We tried everything, and when eventually, weight of numbers pushing and pulling got her in, she went so crazy as soon as it moved, climbing the walls and crashing to the floor, that we had to let her straight out again. The partnership couldn't possibly work, as I wanted to go to shows almost every week. I admitted to myself that Cindy and I really weren't suited, and I broke down in my friend's arms, sobbing that I just wanted my Baloo back. I was lucky to find a very good home for Cindy with some people who would never, ever ask her to go inside a trailer. They ran a very caring riding school and came to fetch her in a horse-box that was so big she didn't even realize it was a horse-box. They told me that she was in fact a twelve year old, not eight years old as I'd been led to believe. It was hard to accept that someone would take advantage of my grief-ridden state to sell me a totally unsuitable horse, but that wasn't the only time it happened. At least Cindy's story had a happy ending and five years later I met her again at the riding stables, and found her to be a very well fed, contented horse. So, I like to think I was meant to come into her life just to make sure that she ended up where she was meant to at that stage of her life.

Months later I tried again, and was conned yet again. I bought a beautiful, apparently faultless Anglo-Arab called Kerrunder. This was a bit of a departure for me as Baloo and Cindy were both cobs, but I was getting desperate to find a suitable horse to get my life back on track. He was very quiet for such a classy horse, so I thought we'd be fine. He was the darkest, glossiest bay and beautifully formed, like a china statue. He loaded into the trailer perfectly, was calm in traffic and he jumped well, so it looked great. The next day I had a bit of trouble, which made me suspicious. I went out and caught him in the field at the yard, but I couldn't get him to come in without putting a bridle on him. Later on, in the opinion of those with more knowledge than me, we thought perhaps he had possibly been kept from water when I'd tried him, which would have had the effect of tranquilizing him. It was true that when we reached the yard on the day of his delivery, he had downed two whole buckets of water. I got over this incident with some masterful handling and for a few weeks things were fine.

Then one summer's evening I was in the schooling arena, and uncharacteristically, Kerry was refusing to jump. Not only did he seem very unwilling to leave the ground, but he also started staggering around. He was behaving so strangely that I decided to get off and take him back to his stable. I spent a sleepless night wondering what on earth could be wrong with him, but the next day he seemed fine, so I rode him as normal, thinking he must have knocked his hind leg the day before and made it feel numb. The next day my friend Jan, came back from a ride very puzzled. She told me that she'd been in the grass field we usually cantered round, and her lemon and white pony, Willum, had been wound up by the sound of another horse cantering in the next field, on the other side of the thick hedge. He'd carted Jan off, and she was unable to stop him. The unseen horse kept pace and Jan panicked a bit because they were nearing the end where there was a gap, and she thought Willum, who was neighing in excitement, and the other horse, were going to collide at the turn. Then Willum suddenly stopped of his own accord a few yards from the gap. There was no sound. Jan rode cautiously through the gap. There was no other horse.

It was Baloo again – we both knew it. Willum had been his best friend. Jan and I talked about it. While it was a wonderful thing that Baloo was revisiting us, we had to ask why he was doing it. He'd come before it seemed, just before I discovered Cindy's problem. Maybe he was trying to warn me about my new horse too. I decided not to take any chances and I called in the vet to get Kerrunder examined. He gave me terrible news. The horse was what's called a 'wobbler'. He was suffering from cervical vertebral stenotic myelopathy, which produced spinal cord compression at the neck level. He would have been born that way. There was no available treatment at that time, and he would have to be retired. Rest would make him safe for a while, and obviously that was how I had been duped by the dealer I bought him from. He'd been rested for weeks before I tried him and the fault hadn't showed up. The problem was that once he was in work you'd never know when it might cause him a problem, from one day to the next. The vet said it was an incredibly dangerous condition, and had I been riding along the road when he suffered an attack, or galloping over fences, the result could have been fatal for both of us, as horses with this condition have no control over their movement when the compression happens.

I was devastated but also a little elated, because I now I knew for sure that Baloo had come back both times to warn me of danger. I had to come to terms with parting with yet another horse, and I was lucky again, to be able to find someone to take him. I started to be concerned that I'd ever find a horse Baloo would approve of.

Luckily a golden boy came to my rescue. Sky Walker was a 15.3hh, chestnut, Welsh cob, with an aristocratic lineage. He was three years old when I fell in love with him as I had never fallen for a horse before – since Baloo. He was owned by a similar sort of person I'd bought Baloo from – not exactly a traveler, but from the same down to earth ilk. Sky had been broken to harness but only briefly sat on a few times. However, he was compliant, if a little timid and had at least seen traffic.

I adored him from the first moment I saw him. Sky was a beautiful bright chestnut, with a flaxen (blond) tail and a thick red mane. He had three white socks and a pretty white stripe that wound its way right down his nose to a pink patch at the bottom of his muzzle.

I had taken a confident friend with me to try him on the road, as I wanted to make sure he was fine in traffic, but wasn't sure I could do it myself. I knew he would be able to jump because the vendor told me that when he was being rounded up in Wales as a yearling, he had jumped out of the corral, over a five-bar gate. When I sat on him I was delighted to feel a willing spirit under the inexperience and a very healthy respect for humans. This meant I'd be able to indulge myself and baby him a bit, without him becoming too cocky.

I took Sky home and then waited with some trepidation to see if Baloo would reappear with another warning. It felt so right, surely he wouldn't. I felt totally at home with Sky, which was a bit surprising as he was only a baby, and very 'green', which can normally be a bit unnerving. I really felt my broken heart might be mended after all if I could keep him. No-one at the yard came in with any strange tales of madly galloping, ghostly horses to recount, and it seemed Baloo wasn't going to say no this time. But I was still a bit worried. I needed my first love's approval before I would feel completely safe. I didn't want to fall totally in love with

Sky if there was going to be an insurmountable problem with him, and I trusted Baloo to let me know the truth. Was Sky the one for me or not?

I got my answer, and it was given brilliantly. One late summer evening I was alone with Sky in the enclosed, barn-type stable yard. I had tied a full net of hay up in the end pen, because I had some serious grooming to do on Sky's abundant tail, and there was more room in there. I was going to tether him, with the hay net to amuse him while I tackled his tail. Before I went to fetch him I got lost in thought, thinking of how I missed Baloo, but how with Sky, finally, I might find peace and fun again. I was wondering, would Baloo give me a sign as he had before, and would he be able to make it one that was obviously positive this time? I mused as I sat in the end pen on a straw bale, gazing mindlessly at the dangling hay net, while Sky waited in his stable.

It was quiet, and Sky made no sound. I could hear an owl outside, and I was enjoying the solitude of being there, just me and my horse, all the others being out in the field on that warm night. Then I felt a shiver, a surge of some energy, a little like electricity in the air. The back of my neck tingled, and the hay net started moving. Hay nets make a very characteristic movement when a horse is eating from them. The net is pushed back as they grab some hay, then swings forward as they tug the hay loose, then it swings back as they let go again. This is what the hay net was doing. While no hay was being taken, the net did its normal back and forth, jerky movement, over and over again. There was no doubt a horse was eating from it. But there was no horse. There was no breeze, no doors were open. I sat transfixed, watching the hay net move for over five minutes. "Baloo?" I breathed. The hay paused in its swinging and I felt a puff of warm, sweet hay-scented breath on my face. I knew instantly that everything was going to be fine this time. A soft snuffing whinny came from the stable and tears poured from my eyes. I got up and ran back to Sky, throwing my arms around his neck. I never heard from Baloo again.

Eventually Sky gave me enough confidence to ride on roads again. He was the most incredible horse. Right from the start we were a team. It took me four years before I took him on roads, because I knew I wasn't ready and horses are so sensitive that I would have transferred my fear to him. I don't know if I would have plucked up the courage by myself, but it was forced upon me. One day we were on a sponsored ride. This was a mapped ride of about 15 miles, you ask people to sponsor every mile and the proceeds go to charity. I agreed to do it because the organizers had promised that it was all off road. What we didn't know until it was too late was that due to exceptionally heavy rain the week before, the fields were water-logged and some of the ride towards the end had to be diverted along a road.

I was horrified when I realized and didn't think we could go on. I stopped Sky as our allotted route diverged away from fields and traveled alongside tarmac, and stood looking at the traffic. It wasn't a busy road and there was a very wide grass verge running alongside, so we didn't have to go close to the cars. In the end I had no choice other than retracing my steps for about 12 miles, so I went for it. Keeping my right leg on him so that there was very little chance of him moving closer to the traffic, I inched Sky along. It was definitely my rapport with him that got me through. Each step was a milestone in our wall of confidence.

After that day, the world opened up a bit for me again. Sky was never really accepting of big trucks or tractors, but because I trusted and knew him so well, it didn't faze me. When I heard one coming down the lanes, I would just find a convenient gateway or drive to nip into while the vehicle lumbered by. I was confident that he would obey my leg and stay close to the hedge or gate at the roadside. I spent many hours fine-tuning this movement, known as a leg-yield. Sky became a brilliant all-round horse. His native breeding made him tough and determined, and his high knee action and powerful neck crest made him feel like a much bigger horse. We did everything together, sponsored rides, eventing, show-jumping, show classes. I even rode him in the local carnival, for charity, dressing up as a fearsome Arab warrior with flashing scimitar. It was one of those once in a lifetime partnerships that defy reason. The last thing you'd have expected after my terrible accident was that I would regain my confidence through riding an untrained three year old horse who wasn't at all confident in traffic, but that's the way it was.

Throughout his life, Sky wasn't the soundest of horses, and our journey was punctuated with quite a few lay-offs through lameness. He had some very large extra bony areas in his feet, called 'sidebones', which made him susceptible to concussion, and he would get footsore if there was no rainfall for too long and the ground got very hard. One vet even suggested once that I should 'do the sensible thing' and find myself a trouble-free horse, but I wouldn't have parted with Sky for a pot of gold! A horse that you feel so connected to is literally worth its weight in gold.

He won a bucket load of rosettes and trophies for me and shook off thoroughbred opposition to come fourth in his very first one-day-event, scooting round the twisty course in the way that the big-striding horses could not. At one event he even came first and won himself a bag of pony nuts and a trophy. I had never been prouder than when I walked up to receive his prizes.

It was extraordinary to have a horse one trusted so deeply. Our partnership forged its way through quite a few adversities and with him I enjoyed one of the most fulfilling periods of my life. Once I got Ace, she joined in with our adventures whenever she could. I would slip a long line with a loop at the end over her head and she would walk along the lanes right next to Sky when we hacked out. When we reached the fields and green lanes I would slip the lead and horse and dog would run joyfully side by side. It was one of the best of times.

CHAPTER 19

Share the Energy

So, by today I've learned an awful lot about my animal soul mates, KC in particular. People love to think their dogs are devoted to them, but not many realize that the undeniable devotion they feel between them has sometimes, literally, been there forever. This doesn't apply to every single dog in the world, of course. As with humans, there are new dog souls too, who are just starting their 'dog time' part of their journey, and will continue to learn alongside their human counterparts, possibly for many lifetimes. Some will have been put with highly evolved human souls for their first canine incarnation, in order to speed their progress.

When your dog is one of those special souls that have decided to reincarnate with you, there are usually classic signs pointing to the truth. The dog (or another animal) may appear in a dream before you meet it in its new body, telling you who it is. Psychics may describe the dog that has died and bring you the message that the dog is about to return, as in Ace's case. The dog may bear birthmarks, defects or scars corresponding to marks that your old dog had. When you meet the dog in his new body, there will be instant recognition, and when you take him home he will know the house inside and out, and will look for the toys that used to belong to him in his old body. The dog may look the same, but sometimes it will choose to look completely different. For instance, if your old dog was a large breed and that might cause you problems now because your living arrangements have changed, then the dog will choose to come back as a smaller breed.

One of the main proofs to me that dog's have had more lives

than just one, is the fact that they dream. Look at the interpretations of what dreams really are. Freud claimed that bad dreams (in people) were to allow the brain to regain control over emotions that have resulted from usually recent experiences that caused distress. Freud and Jung both believed that dreams were communication between the unconscious and the conscious mind. Perls said that dreams are projections of parts of the self that have been ignored. The main consensus seems to be that dreams are a way of resolving the events of the day, closing some down, and filing others for long-term memory storage. All this makes perfect sense for people, but what about for dogs? Are dogs constantly wrestling with the events of the day, trying to make sense of them? This could be so, although that in itself would imply a lot more self-awareness than people usually credit animals with. But, if that were the whole mystery solved, then why is it that we can all observe our special dogs clearly dreaming about things that haven't happened to them? KC will often have a nightmare, where she is whimpering and obviously running in fear from something. Or she'll be obviously hunting something when neither of those things has happened to her, not in this lifetime anyway. The only thing that makes sense is that she is dreaming, as I believe we often do, of things that happened in past lives.

A dog that has an evolved soul, one that has incarnated several times, will be different from the ordinary pooch. This will be a dog that seems at times to be almost human, and at times even more than human. Spiritually, dogs can sometimes seem more evolved than humans, and this is because during their canine incarnations they frequently commit to incredible self-sacrifice in order to return to you, a greater sacrifice than most humans would be capable of. Dogs are naturally capable of selfless and unconditional love, and not many of us have known a single human being that altruistic, and certainly humans are not like that 'without exception'. Another sign of some spiritual superiority is in the fact that dogs don't try and own a future or a past that hasn't come, or has gone. In this life, their conscious mind lives only in the moment.

So, if you believe you have a special dog, what can you do to enhance the connection? The best way to develop your bond with your special dog is first of all to recall other lives you've shared. Your dog already remembers all those lifetimes you've been through together, because dogs, like most animals, are consistently tuned into the universe, and therefore have access to all that has been. Once you have resurrected those memories, you'll know your dog in the same way that he, instinctively, knows you. You'll see how he has developed alongside you, and is connected to you.

The next step is what at first hand may appear as telepathy. You need to practice this every day. If your dog is sitting next to you on the sofa, just think about how you would like him to get off. Don't move, but just feel 'uncomfortable'. Think about how you'd really like to stretch out on the sofa, and while you love your dog to be near, you'd like him to move onto the floor for now. If you can really visualize these thoughts, and the connecting switch is clicked between you, then within half a minute your dog will quietly move off the sofa. If your dog is in another room, just think about how you'd like him to come to you. Picture yourself cuddling and stroking him in the way he loves, and within seconds he'll wake from his dreaming and come to find you. Place your dinner within his reach, and yet give out a signal that this dinner is not to be touched. Your dog won't touch it.

This isn't really telepathy, rather, it's communal energy. We're all connected to everything on the planet, and some connections, like that with your special dog, are stronger than most. What you're doing with these exercises is to finalize and fine tune that connection. It's just like tuning your TV into another station. Tune yourself into the energy your dog is sharing with you, and 'create' the behaviour within that energy. Create it as the reality for you and your dog. Every day with your dog will become a voyage of inner discovery.

Your dog can make you a more balanced emotionally, and therefore happier, person. Dogs share their owner's energy. Have you ever noticed that when you feel edgy or nervous, without giving any outward sign of it, your dog does too? If you're feeling tearful, your dog will try and cheer you up, bringing you his favorite toy, or will snuggle down beside you, giving you the comfort of his body close to yours. If you're feeling happy your dog will get excited and playful, his teeth bared in a goofy grin. You can't hide your emotions from your dog in the same way that you can with people. Every day with your dog can become a doorway to understanding yourself.

The great thing is that with a bit of effort you can share that wonderful and amazing talent the animal has to live in the moment. There are very good reasons for living in the moment. Living in the moment means that you don't hold onto grudges, regrets or guilt. You don't keep reliving bad experiences, or agonizing over things that were said to you, or that you said. You don't keep trying to live in the past. You just learn from it and move on. Living in the moment means that you plan for the future, but you don't try to live there. If anything worrying is coming up, you don't pull it towards yourself and go through the trauma many times over before it actually happens. You don't focus on what may or may not happen in the future, and so waste your life. If you don't live in the moment, you're not really living, you're just surviving life. The only moment that's real is the one you're in right now. The future hasn't happened, and may never happen, and the past is done with and gone. You can't bring it back. The only moment you truly own is this one. Living in the moment makes your whole life better whatever your trials and tribulations, and easier to deal with. Dogs have this talent naturally, and you can share the same gift. Every day will become a school teaching you to live every moment to the full, so that there'll be no regrets, ever.

Make a note of your dog's behavior and compare it to how you're feeling. This has to be how you're *really* feeling, emotionally, deep inside. Whatever face you are portraying to the world, this is not the one your dog will pick up on and mirror. For instance, you might be thinking, *I just want some peace so that I can relax,* and yet your dog is being what seems to be naughty, fidgeting, whining, jumping on the furniture, disturbing you. If you think about it, your dog is acting out all the anxieties you're really feeling but aren't admitting to the world. He's displaying all those feelings that are preventing you from relaxing. If you were truly relaxed, then your dog would be too. This helps you to become a balanced person, because if you want a true barometer of your hang-ups and mental state, just look at your dog.

When you have one of these special dogs, you are the source of his energy. We've all heard of endorphins. These are the chemicals that are actually called endogenous opioid biochemical compounds. It's a morphine-like substance that produces a sense of well-being. On top of that, endorphins have even been claimed to lower blood-pressure and help in the fight against cancer. A well-balanced person creates a steady supply of endorphins. Children that live in a well-balanced environment have this supply quite naturally, but as adults we lose the ability, and to a large extent, we also lose the ability to be happy. Unlike humans, dogs never grow out of this ability, and this is why a well-treated, well-loved dog will exude sheer joy. Your dog can retrain you to have the ability to produce a steady supply of endorphins and share the joy that is natural to your dog.

Because you can't lie to your special dog, not even in a very small way, you can't get away with what most people do, most of the time, and pretend to be happy and in control and balanced. The more badly behaved a dog is, it means the more unhappy their owner is, deep inside. But, you can learn to change, and you'll be able to tell by your dog's behavior whether or not you're succeeding.

The way to create endorphins is to start small. Think of several images in your head that signify happiness; for instance a kite, a balloon, a beautiful flower, a sunset, a giggling child. Your dog needs no such tools, but human adults do. Create solid images in your mind, as many as you can, and whenever you feel yourself slipping towards gloom, think of them. This will create a tiny surge of endorphins, and you can build up from this, because the other good thing about them is that endorphins create endorphins. The happier your thoughts are, the more happiness will grow inside you.

When you get up in the morning, as you're showering, picture the happy dog you want to see all day, sharing your balanced energy. Create this story for your day. If you slip, your dog will show you immediately. His behavior will 'pull you up'. If you practice this until it becomes second nature, you'll find that your dog's behavior will radically change. You'll be in tune, and you won't need words between you. As you build a stronger and stronger bond, you'll find that you're literally not allowed to be anxious, fearful, or unhappy around your dog. Being calm and comfortable will become your natural state of mind. You will only create happy stories in your mind, and therefore in your reality. You'll learn to live in the moment. It will become virtually impossible not to. While enhancing your story to the maximum every day, you make a better life for your dog and yourself, and many other better lives to come.

A natural and unavoidable side-effect to all this communication is that you'll soon find your dog will not longer pull on the lead, he'll always come, eventually to just a hand-gesture or even a thought, and in the end you won't even need a lead to control your dog at all. Every day will become the best day for you and your best, forever faithful friend.

EPILOGUE

Animals and the Planet

About sixteen years ago my husband and I stopped eating meat. First, of course, lamb was off the menu. Because we had pet lambs we quickly came to realize that sheep were 'people' too! Each one had its own personality, and its own degree of intelligence. Once we had accepted that fact, we could no longer countenance eating them. Along with the spiritual journey we were taking, came the realization of the wrongness of treating living, intelligent animals as just a source of easy food that could be killed cruelly with impunity. Next in our transformation, beef was off the menu, as there was a field full of the fascinating bovine creatures next door.

Pigs were a different, yet ultimately similar story. On one of our trips to the market, Tony became fascinated with the pigs and insisted on introducing me to each one. Pigs are actually quite close to humans on a genetic level and it shows in their eyes. If you really make eye contact with a pig, you can establish a deep connection, and once that happens, how can you eat it? Pigs can be trained to do everything a dog can do, and we wouldn't consider eating our dogs, so why pigs? The thought of what each of these intelligent animals must go through during their short and sad life is appalling. In many ways it was much kinder in the days when a hunt through the country and rapid dispatch with a bullet were the norm, if you wanted to eat a dead animal.

Soon the only things left on our menu were chicken and turkey, as birds didn't seem so easy to connect with. But I was soon sickened by the sight of truckloads of chickens in crates. Driving along behind one of these mobile battery farms, I was disgusted by the painful sight of their wings being sucked out of the crates by the lorry driving against the wind. While the chickens in the outside crates were blasted continually with cold air, the ones in the middle crates must have stifled and possibly even suffocated. That was the end of eating chicken for us.

Then we became aware of the conditions turkeys are raised in, and the levels of medication they are given in order to survive long enough to be fattened, so before we knew it we were meat free.

I was ridiculed at the time for the way I felt; vegetarianism was a rare regime back then and considered 'flaky'. With people who ridiculed my feelings and bought veal in the butchers I would ask, "If you came across a calf hit by a car, lying dead in the road, what would you do?" They would screw up their faces in horror and pity at this imagined scene. Then I would add, "Would you chop off its leg and take it home for dinner?" The expression of disgust on their faces would show that when they bought food from the supermarket they didn't really want to accept what they were eating. If people want to eat meat, it would be fair that they should kill the animal themselves. At least that way they would show it some respect and not treat it as if it had no more feeling than a bicycle.

The way the world in general treats animals is to a large extent, deplorable. Animals have proven to me over and over again that they have souls, and one day the human race will look back in shame at the way it has treated these noble souls, in much the same way that we now look back in shame at the generations of slavery we once countenanced. There was a time when black people and red people were regarded as 'sub-human', without rights and without feelings. We know now how abominably wrong that was. But now we are treating intelligent and reasoning beasts the same way, as commodities.

This goes all the way from wantonly and thoughtlessly killing what we regard as 'pests', to caging birds in solitary confinement, robbing them of their miracle gift of free flight, just because their pretty plumage, or their sweet song, or their ability to mimic us, amuses us. What agonies must the sociable parrot or budgie go through, living their life out alone, separated from their flock, literally dying of boredom? We use dogs, cats, rabbits, rats, mice, great apes, pigs, almost any animal you can think of to experiment on. Confined, helpless, lonely and frightened, they are put through terrible pain, in experiments which are largely flawed.

What gives man the arrogance to assume that he can treat other living creatures badly? There will be a reckoning some day, on a spiritual and physical level. Back in days gone by people didn't eat meat every day. Chicken was a Sunday treat, and the bird was bought from a local butcher, having been reared on a local farm. Demand was stable and the food chain was balanced. Now people buy chicken by the container load, reared in intensive conditions, sometimes in this country and often from far afield.

Demand has outstripped supply and the food chain is unbalanced. If a meal-size portion is unrealistically cheap in a supermarket, should we not ask why? Should we not wonder how what we're putting in our bodies to form the building blocks of our cells was reared? Intensively reared livestock is cramped, denied freedom to roam, pumped full of chemical medications to make it live long enough to be profitably killed, and often killed inhumanely, in an atmosphere of fear and violence.

One only has to look at experiments carried out by Masaru Emoto on water, to see evidence of this negative impact on our food. In those experiments water samples formed into totally different crystal shapes depending on whether they were stored in an atmosphere of love, or of hate, creating a comparative language of shapes that corresponded to words.

Saying 'grace' over food may be an old fashioned bible-belt sort of idea nowadays, but blessing your food before you eat it has been proven to affect its goodness. It only stands to reason that mistreatment of the food, will have an opposite and equal reaction. So, taking care of our fellow creatures is essential in all aspects of life on Earth. We must unite and we must forge our bond with nature before it's too late for us as a race.

What some people fail to realize is that all the creatures on this Earth are on a journey together. We need to support each other in order that the communal soul of the planet can thrive and survive.

Who knows what stages there are for us to go through beyond our human condition? Do some people retrace their soul's steps back into the animal kingdom or is it all one way traffic, the progress of the food chain, mirroring spiritual progress? People are improved by association with animals, if they treat them with respect. I firmly believe that children brought up to care for and about animals, and to treat them with compassion and respect, won't grow up to be criminals, committing crimes against people, or waging war against oppressed peoples out of fear or greed. The beauty is that once that connection with animals is established, it lasts forever.

There are very good reasons why people should be kind to animals and they aren't just for the sake of human decency. We begin our existence as primitive souls; blank sheets. That new soul is clean and pure; unblemished and open, but that's not enough – souls need to progress. They need to learn, and be colored by experiences in order to grow, and physical existence is the only way they can do it. That's why we come to this earth. There are some things that we can only experience as mortal beings.

I believe each soul starts off divided into many parts – maybe even as lowly as millions of sparks in pebbles. Each pebble is altered by its existence in the world until it's ready to evolve and then it leaves. It passes through many stages on its journey to fulfillment; perhaps next being divided into thousands of blades of grass, and then maybe it will be ready to accept life as an animal or fish, and could next reappear as 2000 tadpoles or spiders. As each tadpole or spider dies, it returns to the soul's base, changed and progressed by its life. When all 2000 are returned, the entire soul will progress further through the animal chain, perhaps as 200 rats or mice. Eventually it progresses through domestic animals until finally it becomes two dogs, two cats or two horses etc.

It was important to me, that last bit about dogs and cats and horses. It's very true that monkeys are probably the most intelligent, but maybe because of their close connection to us through domestication and the partnerships we form with them, dogs, cats and horses are more spiritually attuned to us. The domestication aspect is very important too, I think, as it's vital that the soul fragments learn to be unafraid of humans. How could they ever become what they fear? I would also add dolphins to this group, except that their way of life and environment is so alien to ours that we can't connect in the same way, unless we elect to live under water. People who treat animals thoughtlessly and without compassion are not only being cruel, they are also denying that soul's right to progress up the chain, and in doing so they seriously damage their own soul too.

If only the whole human race would start accepting that all our souls are connected, like it or not, and stop treating our fellow travelers as commodities to be disrespected and allowed to suffer, in the name of profit, this world would start pulling out of the downward spiral it finds itself in.

Even more importantly, things are going to change drastically in the next decade with regard to the energy of this planet, and as the spiritual community grows, we have to hope that it has encompassed enough souls to ensure that the shift happens, (popularly thought to be coming in 2012) with us all intact. We have to reach a stage of critical mass, meaning that the balance will have changed to a majority of spiritual sensitivity, in order to tip the scales, and if we can do that, then everyone on the planet, aware of not, will be switched on to the truth. Our communion and connection with animals will play a large part in the transformation that is coming.

FURTHER INFORMATION

The website of Masaru Emoto, and his water experiments:
http://www.masaru-emoto.net/english/entop.html

Cesar Millan – The Dog Whisperer:
(http://www.cesarmillaninc.com/index.php).

Madeleine Walker – Animal Communicator and founder of The Exchange of Love Philosophy: www.anexchangeoflove.com

Madeleine teaches that our animal friends have often been with us through many incarnations, and that as our lifelong friends through many lifetimes, they have access to parts of our subconscious that we ourselves are too technological to tune into. When an animal 'misbehaves' to the point where the owner feels it necessary to summon help from her, Madeleine's communication with the animal often reveals traumas needing healing, not only in the animal but also in the owner. The pet is often trying to 'flag up' a problem deep-seated within their owner that they themselves might not even have been consciously aware of, until it is brought to their attention.

The words 'an exchange of love', represent the one species' ability to recognize distress in the other, and call attention to it, facilitating healing. This way, one species heals the other. This form of communication works on many levels. First there is the one-to-one link between Madeleine and the animal on a physical and mental level. Madeleine says that all she feels at this point is a giving and receiving of overwhelming love. When trust is established, even the most apparently aggressive and dangerous animal, relaxes, and the energetic communication begins. This can throw up a complicated entanglement of issues, from trauma experienced by the animal in this life, or a previous one, to health issues, to incidents that happened to the owner while they were away, causing them to return home with disturbed energy patterns attached to them. Their energy is sensed by the animals, and then triggers the 'misbehavior', as they react to it. It can also show up past life scenarios enacted with the same animal and same owner that need to be revealed and healed.

Holly Davis – Animal Communicator:
http://www.hollydavis.co.uk/

Ginny Patterson – Animal Communicator:
http://www.hearme-healme.co.uk/

Margrit Coates – Animal Communicator:
http://www.theanimalhealer.com/

Amelia Kinkade – Animal Communicator:
http://www.ameliakinkade.com/

Jane Summers – Animal Communicator:
http://www.talktotheanimals.co.uk/

Rae Ann Kumelos:
www.voiceoftheanimal.com

Learn how to protect yourself from conmen here:
http://www.fraudaid.com/

Psychic artist, June-Elleni Laine's website:
http://www.psychicartworks.com/june-elleni.html

B O O K S

O is a symbol of the world, of oneness and unity. In different cultures it also means the "eye," symbolizing knowledge and insight. We aim to publish books that are accessible, constructive and that challenge accepted opinion, both that of academia and the "moral majority."

Our books are available in all good English language bookstores worldwide. If you don't see the book on the shelves ask the bookstore to order it for you, quoting the ISBN number and title. Alternatively you can order online (all major online retail sites carry our titles) or contact the distributor in the relevant country, listed on the copyright page.

See our website **www.o-books.net** for a full list of over 500 titles, growing by 100 a year.

And tune in to myspiritradio.com for our book review radio show, hosted by June-Elleni Laine, where you can listen to the authors discussing their books.

mySpiritRadio